A MEDLEY OF MEMORIES AND MUSINGS

SEEKING RHYTHM AND HARMONY

DR MARIAMMA KURIAKOSE

Chennai • Bangalore

CLEVER FOX PUBLISHING
Chennai, India

Published by CLEVER FOX PUBLISHING 2025
Copyright © Dr Mariamma Kuriakose 2025

All Rights Reserved.
ISBN: 978-93-67072-12-7

This book has been published with all reasonable efforts taken to make the material error-free after the consent of the author. No part of this book shall be used, reproduced in any manner whatsoever without written permission from the author, except in the case of brief quotations embodied in critical articles and reviews.

The Author of this book is solely responsible and liable for its content including but not limited to the views, representations, descriptions, statements, information, opinions and references ["Content"]. The Content of this book shall not constitute or be construed or deemed to reflect the opinion or expression of the Publisher or Editor. Neither the Publisher nor Editor endorse or approve the Content of this book or guarantee the reliability, accuracy or completeness of the Content published herein and do not make any representations or warranties of any kind, express or implied, including but not limited to the implied warranties of merchantability, fitness for a particular purpose. The Publisher and Editor shall not be liable whatsoever for any errors, omissions, whether such errors or omissions result from negligence, accident, or any other cause or claims for loss or damages of any kind, including without limitation, indirect or consequential loss or damage arising out of use, inability to use, or about the reliability, accuracy or sufficiency of the information contained in this book.

Dedicated to the memory of

Prof A. I. Kuriakose

With Gratitude

to

Dr & Mrs M. P. Mathai, Paul, Milani and Eva—my biased readers.

CONTENTS

Foreword – Medley .... *vii*
Introduction .... *xi*

1. Life is Like That 1
2. Clueless Aboard 13
3. A Lot to Learn 23
4. Medicine is A Serious Job 29
5. Doctors are Human too 41
6. Rodents Run Over Humans! 56
7. We are Just that Way! 62
8. Colonialism Haunts Us 70
9. European Venture 82
10. Visiting the Land of Canaan 111

FOREWORD – MEDLEY

I would like to begin this brief Foreword with a comment on the title of the book – "A Medley of Musings and Memories" which I think conceals its gravity more than it reveals. On reading through the manuscript, it became clearer that the book is not an intermix of disparate items but a magnificently woven web of life; a splendid amalgamation of interrelated components! It is, in fact, a collection of serious meditative reflections and critiques on the varied and complex experiences of a thoughtful physician.

The author, a conscientious and sensitive physician, whose medical practice had been mostly in the rurban area of a district in the central part of the state of Kerala, perforce, had to interact with countless people cutting across religious, class and gender barriers and had to listen patiently to their multi-layered stories. Through those interactions, the physician tried to understand "the individuals, families and the societal substrate they live in," and also "the ever-evolving pattern of human behaviour and power dynamics in societies with particular stress on how gender impacts them." And when, after a fifty-year-long medical career our author, the doctor, opted for a semi-retired life, she was impelled to look back critically and take stock of her total experience. The book on our desk is its natural outcome. In parenthesis, it may be mentioned that rarely do doctors of her ilk attempt such serious retrospection and hence such an endeavour should invite our compulsive attention.

Dr. Mariamma makes only a very modest claim about her accomplishments and also about what she attempts in the book. "I make no claim of exceptional brilliance or sense of history. My thoughts and observations are those of a lay person as far as religious, philosophical and professional fields, except that of medicine are concerned", she confesses. She also states that she is only using her personal and professional experiences in the process of understanding and assessing the people, their behaviours and the events they consequently generate.

The book covers a variety of issues relating to domestic life, the role of gender in medical education, medical practice, societal relations and in life of faith, etc. and when Dr. Mariamma argues out her views and perspectives on socio-religious issues, she displays the diligence of a sociologist and a social psychologist and maintains the critical rigour of a sane and sober feminist. The tone and tenor of her writing are subtly argumentative and displays the dexterity of a skilled writer, though the fact is that the Medley is her firstling.

I would like to invite the attention of the readers to one of the most significant contributions of Dr. Mariamma as a research-minded physician. We can read about it in chapters six through nine which deal with how she, along with her colleagues, effectively tackled the threat of leptospirosis. It demonstrates how an incisive mind can address even extremely complex medical issues.

As one closely associated with the Malankara Orthodox Syrian Church Medical Mission and Medical College, Kolenchery, where Dr. Mariamma served as a physician for long and rendered dedicated service to the community, I would like to place on record our deep appreciation and indebtedness to her. As an academician, writer, editor and social activist I would like to comment that the present book is a substantial contribution and defies conventional classifications.

I congratulate and greet Dr. Mariamma for making such a contribution.

It is my fond hope that Dr. Mariamma will pursue the path of writing and emerge as one of the major Indian medical writers.

Prof. (Dr.) M. P. Mathai

INTRODUCTION

*I*n the 1960s and seventies, the Illustrated Weekly of India was a popular English weekly. It is now defunct. The editor of the weekly at that time was Sardar Khushwant Singh, a man adept at bringing out controversial and provocative editorials. I was a medical student at the Christian Medical College, Vellore (CMC) at the time and a regular reader of Mr Singh's editorials, articles and stories. A question he raised in one editorial was why there were relatively few women writers and Nobel laureates in comparison to men. I had never been particularly aware of such a comparison or the relevance of such a question in my young life. But once the question entered my mind it refused to leave even while I was kept busy in my personal and professional life. Similar questions have been raised by many other people regarding the poor achievement of women in intellectual and creative fields. My advancing age urges me to gradually ease out of my fifty-year-long medical career and look more closely at the wider world around me. Being semiretired and at the tail end of a generally satisfying medical career I can look back on myself and the society I am part of somewhat more dispassionately than I could at a younger age.

The natural tendency of a teaching clinician when he/she retires is to write a textbook of clinical medicine. There are too many textbooks of clinical medicine in circulation already and I need not add to the list. Putting down my thoughts and memories briefly seems to be more appropriate because the voices raised by ordinary women like me may inspire more women to speak out and thus alter some cliched narratives about women. I am sure there are many women out there who want to tell their stories but are held back by diffidence. I do not claim exceptional brilliance or sense of history. My thoughts and observations are those of an average layperson as far as religious, philosophical and professional fields except that of medicine are concerned. All I can admit to is using my personal and professional experiences as a yardstick to understand events and people around me.

The prevalent narrative of women's intellect and how women feel or act is often an exaggerated, caricatured, stereotyped and misrepresented one made from superficial observation to serve the agenda of female denigration. This deliberate trivialisation continues because ordinary women generally fail to speak for themselves. Perception of women by both men and women is coloured by popular narratives that still prevail because counternarratives are few. The only remedy for this gross misrepresentation is to have ordinary women speak for themselves. Our ordinariness mandates us to express our thoughts and opinions loud and clear.

In this context, I have tried to understand the ever-evolving pattern of human behaviour and power dynamics in societies with particular stress on how gender impacts them. My attempt involves a process of looking back on my own life and recapturing some memories, experiences, ruminations and thoughts over seventy years of life as a female with average knowledge of history, politics or philosophy. The memory of Mr Singh's editorial is an added stimulation to my effort.

Terms like sexism, misogyny and male preference occasionally creep into my narratives because they impact all aspects of a woman's personal and public life. I have witnessed and experienced sexism and misogyny in some measure because they are so pervasive that no woman can completely escape them. My thoughts and musings too are coloured by my gender as a result of this fact. I shall try to examine the role of sexism and misogyny specifically in the fields of science and medicine at different times and places in human history citing examples in later chapters. Admittedly there are other divides and discriminations prevalent in all societies that should be addressed but cannot be scrutinised in detail here. The fields of STEM and medicine are of particular interest to me because of my professional familiarity with them. Areas like politics, literature, law, defence, etc., are relatively unfamiliar areas to me.

My practice has been in the semi-rural area within Ernakulam district of Kerala which is a small state in India. But I have had the opportunity to work to my satisfaction as a diagnostician and physician mostly with the close co-operation and well wishes of the populace. I was also in the right place at the right time to detect the re-emergence and strong presence of the forgotten disease leptospirosis in the farming community of Kerala. Our team ventured into the surrounding rural areas to study the epidemiological aspects of the disease and to learn firsthand the life and occupational practices in a considerable segment of the surrounding countryside. We could also observe the social atmosphere of rural Kerala and the roles played by the two genders during our visits. Over the years I have also had the opportunity to interact with countless people as their doctor, cutting across class and gender barriers and listening to their stories. Through this, I have tried to understand individuals, families and the societal substrate they live in. This is also a process of understanding my own interaction with the society I have been a part of.

Like other ordinary women, I have also played the different roles of daughter, sister, wife, mother, grandmother and physician. My gender is obviously relevant to all these roles, even to my professional identity. Personal experiences that left vivid images in my mind while performing my different roles are briefly described in these pages. I have also cited some simple clinical cases to highlight the importance of effective communication with patients and colleagues as well as of following up on these interactions and the valuable leads they provide. These simple cases are of greater challenge to a clinician rather than the complex ones. I have also put a few of my personal life experiences and random thoughts about the power dynamics operative in the society around me and how I have navigated through it as a member of the gender deemed secondary.

CHAPTER 1

LIFE IS LIKE THAT

*M*y family was an ordinary Nasrani family in a small hamlet in Pathanamthitta district, Kerala. Our family owned a few acres of land in the hilly area where all food items except rice were cultivated. A variety of rice suitable for dry land could be grown once a year, but never enough to feed the family year round. We also had small tracts of cashew, arachnut, coconut and pepper as cash crops. Food was never a problem for us, but liquid cash was never plentiful. My father was a small thin man with ascetic habits and no known vices. He worked very hard and greatly valued education and knowledge. Despite having only 8 years of school education, he was exceptionally well-informed. I was told he was expelled from school for pranking a teacher by putting stones under the teacher's chair legs and tripping him. My father had a wealth of stories and poems and I was his chief attentive audience. I can still recite poems he taught me about virtue and knowledge and stories from Indian epics. Looking back, I realise how much this simple unassuming ascetic man steeped in ancient Indian civilisation influenced my world view. He never went to church while my mother was immersed in church activities.

I was the youngest of seven children and was born when my father was in his early fifties and mother in early forties reminiscent of the Malayalam movie "Pavithram" depicting the story of a girl born to a middle aged couple. The birth of a daughter at that age and in those days was not a happy event for my mother. She already had two daughters and daughters, however, loved, were a financial liability as they could be married off only with large dowries. Even after this, the family would have financial obligations on occasions like childbirth, christening, etc. But I grew up aware that I was a joy to my father and older siblings who worried less about later probabilities. My older siblings practically took over my mothering leaving very little caring for my mother to do. I think this combined with a faint feeling of rejection probably resulted in a lack of emotional connect between my mother and me. Our relationship was rather aloof till the time she started losing memory in her early seventies. Then I tried to make amends for the silent resentment I had harboured as the unwanted female child born in her middle age and visited her frequently.

My eldest brother was twenty-five years older than me. The two siblings above me—a sister five years older and a brother nine years older—were my perfect guides and play mates. Our land consisted of a whole hillside with a small perennial stream encircling it on two sides. The land was difficult to cultivate, but ideal for children to explore and run about.

Caste was still a social issue in my childhood. There were two families, the descendants of a harijan who was apparently my grandfather's right-hand man. They were given a good-sized tract of land when my grandfather partitioned his land. The old man's two sons built houses, cultivated their land and did farm work for other people for additional income. They were under no obligation to work for us but still preferred to work for our family for the same wages they got elsewhere. Their children used to play with us when their parents came to help with our farm. I think Christians practised a very diluted kind of segregation then. The workers were served food on the same kind of plates as the rest of us, but they never came inside the house and were given their meals on the veranda. They had a deep attachment to the land and the crops growing out of it. Years later when I got married and went to my husband's house I saw the same connect and allegiance workers had to the land and crops they helped cultivate even though they did not own them. One old helper lyrically described to me how the rice plants rejoiced and smiled when the farmer visited the rice fields. In my husband's family, there was a custom whereby a male child belonging to the workers was left with my mother-in-law to be educated. There were two families helping in farming activities and each had several male children. When one left school a younger one took his place. The child had free run of the house but had to sleep on a mat on the floor. The arrangement seemed mutually advantageous. The child received nutritious food and education and ran small errands when free. If they felt some resentment it was well hidden. Happily, the present generation has found their own paths and now exemplify social upliftment.

I spent my early childhood mostly under the wings of a doting father and older siblings and suffered no discrimination of any kind usually suffered by girl children in conservative Christian households. I think my two older sisters were not so fortunate.

It was a happy childhood despite financial constraints until the catastrophic happenings in my family later. I was never made to feel undervalued because of my gender either at home or my school.

My world turned upside down by the time I reached seven. My second brother John got married as arranged by the family to a shy and gentle-looking girl. But in a few months, she became a violent (to me) fearsome person. Apparently, she was known to have a mental illness with periodic violent mania. Marriage was supposed to cure her of this.

The family was devastated and guilt-ridden because they felt proper inquiries were not made about the girl before arranging the marriage as the proposal was brought by one of our relatives. I do not remember any treatment details, but remember the commotion in the house while she was made to swallow her medicines. This was a difficult process requiring three strong people two holding her down and one giving the medicine. I used to watch the scene with trepidation. On one such occasion, she head-butted my brother who was holding her down at the head end. He cried out in pain and fell while the girl screamed in wild excitement. He had strangury and haematuria (blood in urine) for several days. This was the last straw for him and he decided to divorce her.

The legal process of divorce was simple because mental illness before marriage was proven, but the Church did not allow divorce under any condition at that time. My brother was excommunicated and our tradition-bound community as a whole disapproved of our family. Even I, all of seven years, was subjected to angry comments and looks but I secretly thought my brother was fully justified. It took him years to recover from the experience. The superstitious belief that marriage cures mental illness persists in society. That poor girl and my brother were both victims of this foolish idea.

The excommunication was lifted later and my brother became a successful small-scale businessman and was respected in the same church and community. He married and became a loving husband and father after some years. He also used to contribute generously to the same church when they needed funds.

A great calamity happened four years later. My eldest brother Mathew was the teller at the State Bank of Travancore, Kozhenchery. He was married to a teacher and had two children with one more on the way. He lived with his family in Kidangannoor about five kilometres away from Kozhenchery. Joseph, youngest of my four brothers, my mentor, emotional anchor and playmate, had just secured a job in the same bank and was to join duty the next morning. He was to stay overnight with Mathew in Kidangannoor and accompany him to the bank the next morning. It was July 1960, a time of heavy monsoon showers. River Pampa was overflowing and the long tracts of paddy fields and the canals flanking the fields extending up from the river bed were flooded. My brother's house in Kidangannoor overlooked the rice fields. It was early afternoon and children were playing on the road along the flooded canal and field. My young brother waded in to join them and fell into the canal and sank. The older one watching from the front yard ran into the rescue and both drowned.

This tragedy ended the happy days of my childhood. My family went into a period of decline and depression. My mother never recovered from the shock and lost the sharpness and vitality she possessed before. She developed dementia in her early seventies and died before reaching eighty. The rest of the family too took time to accept reality. The house was mostly silent with very little interaction among the family members. I was eleven years old at the time and carried the grief right into my adulthood. At school, I felt dazed and could not concentrate. I think the teachers who knew my family promoted me from class to class out of kindness and not because of my academic merit.

My story is also an example of how a good teacher of intuition and kindness can transform a child's life. When I reached class ten, a young teacher Mrs Eapen joined the school and took charge of our class. She was enthusiastic, chatty and very perceptive. The whole class liked this friendly teacher. She took notice of me sitting apathetically in a corner at the back and made me sit in the front seat closest to the teacher's table. She probably knew my family history. She would ask me questions in most classes. I had to pay attention in class and started enjoying the attention. My concentration and studies improved and I finished school as the topper. Among the many people I feel grateful to in my life she is the foremost. I was too young and tongue-tied to express my gratitude, but I hope she understood how she helped an unhappy girl break out of depression. Years later in her eulogy at my brother John's funeral, she mentioned how proud she was of me. It must have been a satisfying challenge for a young and fresh teacher to bring a young girl out of her shell–I am part of her success story.

The family was not sure what to do with me when I finished school. I was only fifteen and too young to be married off. College education was too expensive and my father was not in a position to finance it. He was old, not strong or money-wise. My older brothers had started shouldering financial responsibilities by the time I finished school. Girls in my position usually went in for nursing or teacher's training course (TTC). Only a few went on to college, graduation and a B Ed (Bachelor of Education) to become high school teachers like Ms Eapen. The boys usually went into one of the defence services or learnt typewriting to find clerical jobs in Bombay. The general consensus in the family was to send me for nursing which would enable me to work abroad later and become prosperous. There were several examples of families that had sent their girls to study nursing and became affluent from their foreign earnings. Here events intervened on my behalf.

My third brother George had become an extension officer in Tamil Nadu government service. He was transferred to Vellore and there got married to Rachel, a pharmacist working in CMC (Christian Medical College) Hospital, Vellore. He admired and was inspired by the history, atmosphere and work of CMC. My performance in school had impressed him and he came forward to finance my studies out of the not so large income of his growing family.

In close-knit Indian families after a son gets married his wife struggles to detach him from the mother-in-law whose attention is solely focused on her family. The mother-in-law is often demonised as the villain in a newly married girl's life. But I think most of the blame for the conflict should go to the social system that shrinks a married woman's world to her domestic space and immediate family. In conventional Indian families, there is extreme exploitation of the woman in her role as wife and mother. She is expected to be the family's care giver and maid without personal identity, interests or pursuits. A son is the object of his mother's special love and nurture in this male-centric society even after he attains adulthood. When he gets a partner, the mother starts to feel superfluous and her sense of being excluded from his life leads to conflicts. The groom's sisters too often resent the intruder.

I was too young to be aware of interpersonal dynamics in the family when my two older brothers got married. I was fifteen when George married Rachel. The age gap between us was only twelve years but Rachel treated me like her own daughter. She probably sensed my need for maternal warmth at that vulnerable age. I am not sure how my real mother felt because she did not voice her feelings before me. It was Rachel who made greater efforts to encourage me in my academic pursuit than my brother. This remarkable lady has continued to give me her unconditional support in all my endeavours to date.

I enrolled in Pre-Degree (PDC) science group at St Thomas College, Kozhenchery, some twelve kilometres away from my home. I was to be a day scholar and stay with the family of my eldest brother Mathew who was no more. It was my sister-in-law's mother who took me under her wing and was very kind and caring. She was the widow of a freedom fighter who had died in Burma as a soldier in Subhash Chandra Bose's Indian National Army(INA). He was lost while fighting the British army in Burma, leaving his young widow to look after his aging parents and little daughter. She was a devoted Christian who found great solace in her religion and the courage to support her daughter who was widowed by my brother's demise. The college at the time had no hostels and toward the latter half of my second year, I found accommodation at the YWCA hostel close to the college. My persistent memory of this hostel is being hungry all the time. It may have been because I was sixteen and growing fast. The other inmates were all working women and probably found the food adequate.

My late brother's house as I already mentioned was in Kidangannoor about five kilometres from my college. There were a few KSRTC (Kerala State Road Transport Corporation) buses plying between Kozhenchery and Kidangannoor, but they were always crowded. I preferred to walk the distance. It was on these walks that I met a very gentle and unassuming girl, another Rachel who was in the same PDC batch, but in a different group. Rachel's father worked in KSRTC and she had season tickets, but she preferred to walk with me to and from college.

Rachel was an avid reader of Malayalam classic novels and our walks involved her narrating to me the plots of stories she had read. In my case, I was introduced to old English classics by the college librarian. Rachel and I would go to the library together and stand silently before this slight old man with prominent teeth. I think he was happy to see us entering his silent kingdom because we did not see many students visiting the library. He would make an entry into the register and hand Rachel a Malayalam book and me an English one. He chose the books and we took them silently. This was a weekly routine and no words were spoken on either side. I remember reading The Water Babies, Jane Eyre, Oliver Twist, Far from the Madding Crowd, Wuthering Heights, etc., at this gentleman's silent directive. Rachel graduated and joined the secretariat and retired as assistant secretary. I visited her home in Trivandrum later. She was as unassuming and gentle as I remembered. I feel grateful for the friendship of this gentle girl and our long storytelling walks and always remember her with affection. She passed away after an illness a few years ago.

The transition from Malayalam medium in school to English medium in college was a little difficult. However, my brother had greater confidence in my intellectual abilities than I had. He encouraged me to study hard and I tried to do my best. I passed with distinction and was urged by him to apply for the MBBS course in CMC. It may be that he wanted to give me an opportunity he had wished for, but was denied the chance by circumstances.

Becoming a doctor sounded great and I sent my application to CMC. However, I had no grasp of what it involved and how to prepare for the entrance test. I don't know if there were guides or training centres for entrance tests in 1966. If there were, we were not aware of them. A cousin of mine had gifted me a general knowledge book. This book and my PDC textbooks served as my study material for the entrance test.

The written test was in Kottayam and I wrote it without much hope of selection. To my surprise, my sister-in-law Rachel in Vellore wrote to inform us that my name was listed among the 120 candidates chosen for interview on the notice board and that the letter calling me for the interview would arrive shortly. Out of the 120 candidates 60 would be selected. I waited hopefully for the interview card that never came. The following days were strange. Rachel checked with the college office again and wrote back my name and number were definitely there and the office was sending me another card. When this card also failed to appear the college apparently sent a telegram at Rachel's request, which also failed to reach me. Informed thus Rachel wrote back by registered post urging me to come to Vellore forthwith since there was no time for further back and forth. The postman usually delivered my family's post at the house of an uncle living half a kilometre away to avoid the walk to our house. No one questioned the postman or the post office, let alone the uncle. The mystery of the missing letters and telegram remains unsolved to this day.

It was decided that my father and I would board the train from Tiruvalla to Katpadi (the nearest railway station to Vellore) the next day and reach Vellore early in the morning on the day the interview began. That evening three relatives came to our house and told my father not to take a young girl, hardly seventeen, to such a faraway place. My father, usually very receptive to their advice, rejected it this time and we boarded the train the next evening from Tiruvalla. I still wonder if it was real concern for my safety or just malice on the part of these uncles.

We reached Katpadi railway station early next morning. My brother was waiting at the station. He took us home to freshen up and Rachel took me to the medical college office to register for the interview.

Entering the CMC Medical College campus for the first time was an enchanting experience. The campus was quiet, lush and shady in contrast to the hot, dry and dusty Vellore landscape around. It was a green forest dotted with stately old stone buildings blending well with the verdant surroundings. Flowering laburnums, acacias and gulmohar trees added colour to the green background. I remember there were a lot of bushes bearing a profusion of purple flowers around a large residential building near the entrance. For some reason, they were called "bachelor's tears". On my last visit, I looked for these flowers and the bushes had all disappeared. One assumes the bachelors in CMC are no longer shedding tears. But otherwise, the colourful vista remains somewhat the same today as when I first saw it fifty-odd years ago. On my occasional visits to CMC, this campus makes me feel nostalgic about my youthful days.

CHAPTER 2

CLUELESS ABOARD

The final selection process in CMC has apparently changed recently. In those days the process was a three-day long interview. The candidates were divided into groups supervised by two doctors of the same gender as the candidates. Person-to-person dialogues, questions and group activities were all part of this process. At the conclusion, everyone was assembled in the central courtyard called Sunken Garden built around a pond. The registrar announced the chosen candidate's names and numbers. To me, it was rather like my idea of the apocalypse when an angel would call out the chosen one's names and leave the rest to purgatory. This public proclamation was a traumatic experience for those not selected as it was thrilling for those selected. To my surprise, my name was called out too. My feeling was a mix of relief and pride. I believe I cried. There was also lurking anxiety about my lack of sophistication and classroom English that sounded stilted among the fluid-spoken English I heard around me.

The next obstacle was the red-tapism of Kerala University. My selection was based on the entrance examination and interview results but Madras University registration for students required the mark list of the qualifying examination and transfer certificate both of which were delayed by the university. I was given an ultimatum by the college. It required direct visits to Trivandrum by Rachel's brother to persuade the university to issue the certificates. I believe it was actor Mohan Lal's father, a high-ranking official in the secretariat, who intervened to cut the red tape.

Adjusting to my new environment was trying for a time but I gradually got over the unfamiliarity. There was ragging to start with. And it was celebrated like a festival every senior enjoyed and every newcomer dreaded. It involved singing, dancing and any activity the seniors thought funny and could devise for the newcomers. I remember getting very angry at a senior about some matter I can't remember. On another occasion, another senior smacked my bottom which I found demeaning. I don't remember any other unpleasant incidents. Three days of official ragging ended with every newcomer getting dunked in the lily pond without lilies in the sunken garden at midnight. This was followed by singing and dancing around a campfire. It was all part of a great tradition and there were no hard feelings afterwards. In a sense ragging improves camaraderie if indulged in moderation and psychopathic personalities are kept at bay by the authorities.

CMC was to be my world for the next twelve years with a break of two years in between to fulfil my bond in rural hospitals. These twelve years were the most significant ones in forming my worldview and professional attitude. Images of the silent peaceful campus, noisy hostel days, early morning bus rides to the hospital for clinical teaching, eagerly awaited Sunday lunch biriyani all remain unfaded. The Sunday lunches were memorable-steaming moist chicken biriyani with a piece of chicken ladled out on our personal steel plate could not have been exceptional, but I am sure all my hostel mates must remember it as the tastiest biriani they ate in their entire life. Youth and hunger are great tastemakers. There are both happy and unhappy cringe-worthy incidents woven into the tapestry of my mind and I am glad of them all. These experiences enabled me to develop insight into people's attitudes and how to navigate through success, failure, criticism and approbation with equanimity.

At last!

CMC is an iconic institution of excellence in medical education, research and patient care. It was started by the idealistic and visionary American lady doctor Dr Ida Scudder. Ida's parents were working as Christian medical missionaries in Tamil Nadu in the late 19th century. Young Ida was overcome by the appalling state of healthcare available to the villagers, especially the women in the area. The women and relatives would refuse to let male doctors examine sick women or women in labour even in dire circumstances. Some vestiges of this attitude remained in some communities even in the late sixties. (I remember one of my male seniors nearly getting beaten up for asking a woman to expose the skin lesion on her thigh for examination.)

One incident of a woman in labour being denied medical assistance by a male doctor dying in childbirth was the final event that made medical care to the poor villagers young Ida's life mission. She gave up her dreams of returning to America to lead a life of leisure. Instead, she got trained as a doctor in the USA, returned to Vellore and started a single bedded clinic in 1900. Today CMC is one of the foremost healthcare and research institutions in Asia with a reputation for excellence all over the world. It has multiple campuses and students from all over India and several Asian countries study here. Western medical colleges send exchange students to CMC to learn about tropical diseases. CMC's motto "not to be ministered unto, but to minister" remains fresh in the mind of every student trained by this institute [whether they practice it or not is a different matter]. Christ's mission of healing and teaching is taken very seriously here. Being a CMC-trained doctor is a matter of pride for us not because of the prestige value, but the professional attitude and practical experience we gain from the institution. Importance is given to more hands-on experience, becoming responsible and accountable rather than learning a lot of theory which one can anyway learn from textbooks. Students are motivated to serve their society and restrain greed. However, I was sadly disillusioned when a CMC-trained doctor was recently arrested on charges of taking bribes. Another sad fact is that a sizable number of CMC graduates emigrate to Western countries. They must have reasons of their own, but a developing country like India is losing many committed and competent doctors thereby.

One remarkable feature I have admired about CMC is in spite of its very Christian atmosphere there is no proselytisation or attempt to impose Christian faith on students. There were prayer meetings and chapel services one could attend or not attend at one's own will without any kind of compulsion. I was rather irregular in attending these sessions myself. Non-Christians, as students, staff or patients feel equally at home in this liberal Christian atmosphere. Several departments are headed by famous non-Christian doctors. CMC is Christian in orientation and secular in practice.

In my time there were only sixty students in each MBBS batch and the teachers knew every student. They were very approachable and humane. There was an impressive and inspirational array of teachers like Drs James Varghese, Mary Jacob, L B M Joseph, Grace Koshy, Jacob John, Jacob Abraham, Sheila Pereira, Malati Jadhav, Sushil Chandy and V. I. Mathen who impressed me in their own different ways. I am grateful to all of them. Dr Jacob

John and Dr Grace Koshy were of great help to me later when I needed advice and laboratory support to diagnose human leptospirosis in Kerala.

Small student groups were often invited to the teachers' homes for tea and the main attraction for us was the food they provided. In general, these teaching doctors were excellent in their jobs and true to their calling. Their salaries were comparatively low and only the ones who believed in simple living and high thinking stayed back permanently to work in CMC. In fact, the CMC lady teachers could be recognised outside the campus by their inexpensive pastel cotton sarees and unadorned appearance. One professor told me how she was not allowed to look at expensive silk sarees in a textile shop in Vellore. She was there to buy a silk saree for a relative. The salesman was unimpressed and told her she was wasting her time as the sarees were too expensive for her. He clubbed her as an impecunious person because of her inexpensive dressing style. She actually was from an affluent family. This simple lifestyle was a boon to me too because I did not have the money to spend on expensive clothes or ornaments to deck up in style. My brother had to look after his growing family as well as fund my education from his tight family budget. I did not mind my simple appearance at all. I remember one classmate asking me why I did not wear ornaments and better clothes. I probably overcompensated for this lack later subconsciously by developing a deep dislike of finery. My dislike continues even though they have become easily affordable now. My family sometimes objects to my less-than-affluent appearance.

In those days I was naïve enough to think that all teachers were spiritually above base human emotions like jealousy, greed and prejudice. I was sadly disabused of this idea slowly as I became older and wiser. I too became a teacher later in life and remained more or less the same person as I was before. Of course, one's insight improves with age.

Getting acclimatised to this eclectic world was tough for a shy, reclusive and unsophisticated girl like me. But I treasure both happy and unhappy memories of CMC. I had very few friends, but the ones I had were genuine ones. Rupa Solomon, Usha Onden and Jayasree Kidao need special mention. All of them left for foreign lands. Rupa who passed away last year and I used to have great reunions when she visited India. I have lost touch with Usha who was great at boosting my morale whenever it needed boosting. I met Jayashree a few times after leaving Vellore and she is a successful gastro-enterologist.

Is CMC such a paradise of goodness? Any collective human enterprise has drawbacks and CMC is no exception. One cannot totally eliminate factors like nepotism, rivalry, sexism etcetera in a place where a large number of people with varying backgrounds are crammed together and competing and striving for career advancement and excellence. But from personal experience I know these are kept in check by dedicated persons in key positions and the long tradition of transparency.

In general, CMC was egalitarian and gender-neutral to a great extent. But it also reflected the attitudes of the society from which its members emerged. The medical college was started initially to train women doctors, but when I joined there were only twenty-five women in our class of sixty. I don't know the reason because there was no dearth of women aspiring to become doctors. Gender discrimination may have crept into the initial pro-women enthusiasm. Certainly, there was no dearth of brilliant women students. Often the best outgoing students were women.

There were several senior female doctors in some of the departments especially paediatrics, obstetrics and gynaecology (O&G). Preclinical and Paramedical departments were often headed by women. There was poor representation of women in surgical specialities and super specialities supposedly because of the physical fragility of women. But in practice, the most physically challenging speciality O&G was usually an exclusive female domain. Here, I witnessed reverse sexism, where the lone male obstetrician was ridiculed behind his back-a case of "women-will, if they can". I believe the reason for the poor representation of women in surgical specialities is women's reluctance to compete with men who resent the female invasion of their strongholds rather than female frailty. This reluctance is less evident now in the medical community but still exists. Sometimes I regret not entering a surgical field instead of internal medicine because I was gifted with steady hands and enjoyed the few chances I got to carry out minor surgeries during my internship. I get vicarious satisfaction from my daughter's choice of surgical speciality.

In the classroom, there were whiffs of unstated male superiority. Any decisions as a class were made by the boys. The girls, anxious to please and respectful, concurred sweetly even while silently disagreeing. If a girl openly disagreed she was marked as arrogant and bossy. Being unaware of this male-female divide I must have displeased some male stalwarts.

There were a few Sri Lankans and Malaysians who were generally two or three years older than students from Indian schools and colleges. They were more westernised, brash and dominated the class. Other students always tried to be in their good books. Indians in general and Malayalees in particular were more subdued. Public school English accent was much admired and Malayali accent held in ridicule. Malayalees who studied in Kerala and had Malayalee accents were said to be from the backwaters in good humour (backwaters are now considered the most beautiful feature of the Kerala landscape). Hopefully, this attitude may have changed as new generations of Indians free themselves from the immediate postcolonial inferiority complex and language chauvinism of their predecessors. Accents are always influenced by the language one hears from birth and I see no shame in any accent as long as speech is decipherable and structurally correct.

Two incidents remind me of the subtle male superiority equally persistent in the male and female psyche. During our internship (practical training) a Sri Lankan boy (call him C) and two of us girls were allotted patients in the same ward together. We girls would dutifully work up the patients allotted to us and C would appear when the doctor in charge came for ward rounds. One day the doctor wanted to discuss a particular patient. There was an uncomfortable silence. The doctor looked at me expectantly and I blurted out it was C's patient. C was evidently very angry with me. I think the doctor who was a Kashmiri Hindu, was intimidated by C's looks and moved on to another patient without comment. My girl colleague took me aside later and advised me to be very careful in dealing with boys like C because they could make life very difficult. It did not impress me very much since I was obviously unpopular and life was tough anyway.

During our Labour (Delivery) room posting the girls were expected to groom and serve the patient while the boys had to come just when the actual delivery happened. The nursing students usually did the preparation of patients for our male colleagues probably for reasons of modesty. One patient allotted to me needed a caesarean section delivery. The lady obstetrician in charge assured me to my joy that I would be her first assistant. I considered it a great privilege and profusely thanked her. The surgery started. The surgeon stood on the right side of the operation table and I was on the left as the first assistant. A male intern stood on the side of the surgeon as the second assistant who would hand her the instruments, swabs, etc. As the surgery proceeded I had to stand and watch as the surgeon made the male intern assist her from the wrong side awkwardly. When he pointed this out she was unfazed and attributed this to her forgetfulness. I thought this was a lie and she merely wanted to please the male intern. To his credit, he was not particularly pleased. Minor incidents like this show up the male preference in female minds.

CHAPTER 3

A LOT TO LEARN

The MBBS course took six years during which one gained firm basic knowledge of human anatomy and physiology. Clinical competence comes only with years of actual practice. But becoming a doctor is in itself thrilling. Doctors in those days were expected to perform miraculous cures and were considered to be godlike in the poor communities around Vellore. But this was not so in Kerala where patients were less adoring and more demanding.

During the internship, we had a three-month posting in remote rural hospitals some of which had no experienced seniors and we were left mostly to our own devices. I also had a two-year stint in two remote rural hospitals in Kerala as part of my bond. I had to manage with my lack of practical experience and without supervision. This made for many adventures –some happy and others not so but all of them interesting. CMC provides excellent training to its students, but MBBS is only the first stepping stone to a career in clinical practice. It cannot equip the student to deal with the many practical problems and emergencies that arise.

Several incidents happened during my rural wanderings over two years as a young inexperienced female doctor that remain etched in my mind. Two incidents, one in Kerala and one in Nagari, narrated here are memorable not because of the rarity of the cases or brilliance on my part but because I want to pay homage to the surgical textbook Bailey and Love (B&L), my all-time favourite medical book. B&L is a simple and lucidly written surgery textbook for medical undergraduates and I remain an ardent admirer. It is the only medical textbook I have read from cover to cover more than once. I would advise all budding doctors to do the same.

My first posting during my internship was in Nagari, a backward area in Tamil Nadu, Andhra Pradesh border. A doctor couple was working in the hospital, but I think they were overworked and preferred to leave interns from CMC to deal with whatever problems the budding doctors came across. One day while managing the outpatient clinic by myself a teenage boy came with fever, throat pain and difficulty in swallowing for a few days. He was in obvious distress. Examining his throat showed swelling on one side of his throat in front of where the tonsil should have been. It was almost blocking off the pharynx making even breathing difficult. It was a dramatic first demonstration of a peritonsillar abscess (quincy) for me and the only thing to do was to open and release the pus. I knew if I made a cut the wrong way I could paralyse his palate. There was no one I could ask for help (mobile phones had not arrived back then and even landlines were difficult to access). Then a diagram I had seen in B&L of quincy incision presented itself to my mind. I made an unsure cut with the tip of a scalpel. The boy coughed and spat out pus and actually cried in relief. I was equally relieved but did not cry.

My first rural posting in Kerala was to an underdeveloped village in central Kerala. The people were simple, poorly educated rural folk. There was no other nearby hospital. I think they were happy to have some kind of medical help, even that of a young inexperienced female doctor. The second posting was in a slightly more urbanised area also in central Kerala. The transition to urbanisation may have made the local population unsettled. The hospital had only two auxiliary nurse midwives and one helper, all females. There were always a few drunkards hanging around the hospital and passing rude comments to the all-female staff. On my first day of duty, there was a small meeting to bid farewell to the male doctor who owned a motorbike and was apparently popular with the local elite. It was also to welcome me as the new doctor. The person who made the speech made appreciative comments about the departing doctor. All he could say to welcome me was unlike the departing doctor, the new doctor was not capable of visiting patients at home on a motorcycle in the middle of the night. He said what could not be prevented had to be tolerated. This patronising comment made all the listeners snigger.

During my first posting in the small remote hospital in central Kerala mentioned above I had a very distressing experience. An unconscious child was rushed into the hospital with a crowd following. Apparently, the child was playing and suddenly started to struggle to breathe and fell unconscious. The child was brought in limp and struggling to breathe spasmodically. The possibility was a foreign body in the airway. Compression of the abdomen proved useless. There was no foreign body in the upper airway as far I could make out and there was no way of examining the lower airway. I had no help or equipment and even if I had I would not have known how to use them. I tried putting in a large bore needle between the lower tracheal rings to let in air. This had no effect and I stood and watched helplessly as the child stopped breathing. I still wonder if I failed to do a proper Heimlich manoeuvre that could save the child in that emotionally charged atmosphere.

The following incident, which I came across, took place in the same central Kerala hospital mentioned above—a young man was brought in with a calf wound caused by a broken soda bottle. The sister on duty called me to suture the clean-looking superficial wound. Swabbing the wound prior to suturing I was shocked to see something large and white stuck inside. I was looking at the severed tendon of the large calf muscle that helps to flex the foot. I had never seen a cut tendon of any size before and this was really a large one. I felt helpless and wanted to send the patient away. The sister was made of sterner stuff. All the nurses in this hospital only had a short diploma training but they had formidable experience and attitude in dealing with doctors and patients. The sister assisting me assured me sweetly there was nowhere I could send him to nearby and I had to do my best.

I started hesitantly and looked for the lower end of the cut muscle and there was no muscle. Then I remembered that muscles contract and this one must have moved up when freed from the tendon. So, I had to make a long perpendicular incision upward to find the hiding muscle. All this exploration was done under my inexpert local anaesthesia. It helped that the young man was stoic and made no objection and bore up well. I found the missing muscle. The distance between the tendon and muscle end must have been at least two inches. Muscle and tendon had to be brought together first. I did not know how to proceed and tried to remember if I had seen any diagrams of calf muscle suturing. B& L again came to my rescue. A simple diagram in it I hadn't given much credit for showing how the suture should be taken shone bright in my mind's eye and my hands followed the image in my mind. The needle was big enough, but the only thread available was thin catgut. It could not stand the strain of pulling the far apart muscle and tendon close and broke. The sweet sister advised me to fold the thread twice and try again. The same result followed. After the third folding the thread held. Fortunately for us and the young man, the muscle and tendon were not shredded and stayed together and I closed the wound thankfully. Immobilising the foot was our next quest. There was no plaster of Paris. We searched the building and found some small wooden planks we improvised as splints. Strips of old bedsheet used liberally kept them in place. The only available antibiotic, procaine penicillin, was started.

I left the hospital a few days after the adventure and thought no more of it. It was a run-of-the-mill procedure for an experienced surgeon but my inexperience and poor facilities made it a great adventure for me. I happened to meet the doctor who followed up the patient a few months later and was told the leg was fully healed and functional. I wonder how much flak a young doctor would face if this incident happened and things went wrong in today's Kerala with its woke population and media.

Though medical knowledge and facilities have greatly improved over the last decades many such incidents happen in the professional life of a doctor even today. The ones that happen when she/ he is inexperienced and clinical practice mystifying make long-term memories.

CHAPTER 4

MEDICINE IS A SERIOUS JOB

I went back to CMC after two years of rural wandering with hopes of doing post-graduation(PG) in internal medicine. Dr L B M Joseph, head of the department of surgery, had encouraged me to pursue a surgical speciality during my internship in his department, but I lost my enthusiasm for surgery during my two-year stint in rural service. Postgraduate seats were few at the time and competition for branches like internal medicine was very intense. There was no entrance test. Admission depended on performance in MBBS examinations and the general impression one made during the MBBS course and internship. Personal preferences, contacts and favouritism may have played some part in the selection of candidates too. One does not like to go into details that may tarnish reputations. I got a seat in Internal Medicine after an apparently turbulent selection process.

My three years of postings through the different medicine and related departments were a mixed bag. The PG training in CMC is excellent and involves a great deal of practical experience and gradually increasing responsibility. I was the only female student in my batch of four. Some of the postings were wonderful and others harrowing but still great learning experiences. My postgraduate thesis work was guided by Dr Jacob Abraham, the well-known neurosurgeon since the Department of Neurosciences in CMC did not yet have a separate Neuromedicine Department. Dr Abraham with his dry humour and sharp eye for clinical findings was an especially inspiring person. But on the whole, I had a very tough PG training period. Even to this day, I feel a few of the HODs carried a grudge against me and tried to make my postings difficult. The reason may have been that I had replaced an influential professor's special candidate in the tough selection process and my gender. I never confronted them, but it took me a few years to get over my resentment of these senior professors.

My batch mates were representative of our society in their differing attitudes to women in professions. One batchmate was very bright, traditional, hardworking, entitled and very ambitious. He was never openly critical or rude to this sole female batchmate(myself). But when he was getting married I asked him about his bride's occupation and he told me she was not ambitious as if that was her greatest quality. To my slightly paranoid ears it (justified I still feel)sounded like an indirect criticism of my professional ambition. One batchmate was a very sweet person – polite, friendly and free of any prejudice or malice. I rarely saw these students because our postings were always different and we met only during common teaching sessions. We were posted in pairs to different medical units and I was unfortunate to be paired with the most ardent male supremacist I have encountered in my professional life. He could only be described as extremely manipulative. It may have been paranoia on my side, but he seemed to be on a mission to undercut me and make me feel inadequate. I think the challenging time I had with him stood me in good stead for my future dealings with male colleagues with an attitude. (I must admit to attitudes of my own). To their credit, none of them was as obnoxious as this gentleman and several of them were friendly and democratic once we got to know each other. I have reached a stage in life now where I can actually look back on these instances with sympathy and some degree of humour.

I got married in my last PG year and was lucky to have a partner who never tried to interfere with my professional duties. My husband is a structural engineer and professor who was confident and excelled in his own profession and so had no reason to compete with me or trivialise my profession as some husbands of professional women are prone to do. In fact, I think he was proud of me.

I did a six-month stint in CMC after passing and went back to Kerala to my husband's home. Here I got invited to join an upcoming mission hospital in nearby Kolenchery. I joined this hospital named Malankara Orthodox Syrian Christian Mission Hospital(MOSC) in 1980 and was part of its ups and downs for the next forty-one years. Looking after two children and working long hours in patient care was hard, especially in the early years of motherhood. Inspite of domestic help, it was a period of intense stress as I struggled to perform all my different roles. But looking back I think I tried my best to do justice to my roles. At least my children did not complain of being neglected and people in and around Kolenchery gradually became almost like my family.

My two children are responsible citizens and hard-working professionals.

The economic and human profile of Kerala is different from other states in India which have both very rich and very poor people. But in Kerala, there are only a few very rich families. The population consists mostly of lower middle-class families that run on tight budgets and they form most of the patient population of MOSC. My major interaction throughout my career has been with this section of the populace. The poorest go to the very crowded government hospitals. The relatively affluent prefer more expensive corporate establishments. These two groups depend on MOSC only in dire situations.

Kolenchery is in the eastern part of Ernakulam district and was still underdeveloped and rustic in the early 80s. MOSC was established as a fifty-bedded hospital in 1970 by a group of prominent local visionary citizens and headed by two committed people --M. Chacko Pillai, a prosperous retired government contractor as secretary and Dr K C Mammen, retired paediatrician from CMC, Vellore as its director. When I joined the hospital in 1980 it had already grown to 250 beds and had all basic departments. It catered to the health needs of a large rural area of Ernakulam and Idukki districts. Fifty-three years after its inception it has become a medical college hospital with over a thousand beds and all modern facilities training undergraduates, post-graduates and paramedicals. This institution now called Malankara Orthodox Medical College Hospital became the instrument of development and prosperity of the surrounding countryside.

When I joined MOSC the group of doctors working there consisted of half a dozen young and smart doctors all male except for the lady doctor heading the O&G department. They were all good at their jobs and obviously thought well of themselves. Initially, I did not feel welcome into this masculine milieu as a newly minted inexperienced female physician. It was unsurprising for men in a predominantly male domain to resent and resist female intrusion. I think my unapologetic and nonchalant attitude made their wariness more pronounced. The easy way to manage such situations is to act humble and cute which I never could do. I tended to become defensive and assume indifference when discriminated against and agreeable and polite when treated with respect. There were instances when I was made to feel inadequate. However, the ice melted slowly and I was accepted and settled in gradually. In fact, most of them became my friends and helpful colleagues gradually. This was largely due to the moral support of the two insightful and open-minded men at the helm -- Dr Mammen and Mr Chacko Pillai. It was humbling at times to see the way Mr Chacko Pillai dealt with matters of patient care and staff welfare with such concern and humility. He became a highly respected father figure to me.

Recently a colleague of mine, Dr Abraham Mammen described the evolution of patients' perception of doctors over the decades. The description started as Bhagwan (god), went on to Insan (human) and now to Shaitan (Satan). This is especially true of the average Malayali's attitude to doctors. Kerala's perception of doctors is somewhere between human and shaitan.

The social milieu and patients' attitudes to doctors in Kerala are starkly different from what one comes across in CMC. CMC is a world in itself. Both the medical college campus and hospital campus are geographically secluded from the surrounding area. Students and staff come from varied cultures and backgrounds though united in the quest for learning, teaching and healing almost to the exclusion of interests outside medical profession. It is a virtual medical Shangri-La cocooned from the world outside to a great extent even to the extent of being claustrophobic sometimes. Patients come from all over India into this unfamiliar atmosphere in great awe. The employees are mostly protected from the angst and demands of patients and relatives because CMC's reputation justly evokes trust.

Kerala's government and mission hospitals (now there are some exclusive corporate ones.) generally allow open access to the general public. The patient population of all economic strata in Kerala is more knowledgeable, demanding and opinionated compared to the rest of India. While this helps in avoiding exploitation by unethical elements in the medical fraternity there is a negative aspect to it too. Most patients and relatives have access to print and social media and both provide populist, incomplete and often erroneous information. The sense of powerlessness felt during a serious illness frustrates the average person and enhances his resentment towards the treating doctor who symbolises power. Protests, both just and unjust are common. Physical violence against doctors and hospitals is not uncommon.

Even as I write this all hospital staff in Kerala are on strike in protest against the gruesome murder of a young lady doctor in a government hospital in the presence of police and security. It reminds me of a similar encounter I had with a patient while on ward rounds. This was a man brought two weeks earlier to the emergency room in an unconscious state with depressed breathing. He had consumed an organophosphate insecticide in significant quantity. I was on hand to intubate and resuscitate him. Later he was sent to the ward where a male doctor looked after him over the next two weeks. Then one morning he barged into the ward where I was examining patients. He abused me loudly and started brandishing a knife threateningly. He claimed he developed a bed sore because of my carelessness. Bed sores develop because of prolonged bed-ridden state without frequent position change and doctors do not stay with the patient to do the positioning. It is done by the nursing staff and caretakers. I think he was afraid to challenge the male doctor who looked after him in the ward for two weeks and chose a softer target to vent his anger on. I was saved heroically by a clinical assistant named Alias who caught him from behind and disarmed him. This man came to me as a patient some months later. I was unforgiving enough as to refuse to see him.

Doctors and nurses coming out of peaceful though busy CMC find this kind of experience intimidating. I know a brilliant CMC-trained neurosurgeon opting out of practice in Kerala disillusioned. The average Malayalee is a critic and slow to accept and trust doctors. I too found this attitude of partially concealed hostility difficult initially in spite of being eager to start practice after getting my PG degree. I stayed put anyway because my husband's home was nearby and he was a professor in the nearby engineering college. I had two young children and uprooting the family was impractical and cowardly.

The fact that medical practice requires much more than brash confidence and a lot of theoretical knowledge dawned on me gradually. My years in CMC had provided me with skills and attitude but the more important real-life learning and practical approach came by learning from patients I treated over the years in Kolenchery. I realised medical practice needed a lot of common sense, awareness of one's own deficiencies and an open mind. This was especially true for married women doctors because they were considered inefficient and distracted by family matters. The unmarried ones were considered shrewish and eccentric. It was a no-win situation for women doctors except in O&G. The term lady doctor was synonymous with O&G practitioners and they were considered a necessary evil because women did not like being examined by male gynaecologists. Sending a patient to consult a lady doctor meant consulting a gynaecologist. I think women paediatricians too were accepted to some extent. Women internists were few and women surgeons unheard of outside O&G. The attitude toward women doctors in general was patronising.

There was a section of populace I could not empathise with in the beginning. Women of some affluent families in my view seemed supercilious and vain. Most of the ones I met were middle-aged and unemployed with grown-up children. As a rule, they gradually gained weight and developed metabolic diseases. My lack of sympathy must have been obvious, but over the years I understood they were victims of patriarchy, female segregation and empty nest syndrome. I think most of them felt redundant after their children grew up and their husbands became busy with their own activities outside. These women form a reservoir of unused human resources which if organised effectively can contribute significantly to positive social change. I see some of them joining social service organisations and finding life more meaningful now.

One revolutionary scheme that has empowered women of lower socio-economic strata is the Kudumbasree project for women in Kerala. Previously unemployed and dependent women are finding self-employment in areas like food processing, microfinance, agriculture, eateries, etc. They are gaining autonomy and bringing about a silent social revolution.

I learnt to be realistic and accept the patient's mental state and behaviour including sexism to gain helpful information and trust. Social prejudice and misogyny had to be understood and dealt with. I often had to sit with a straight face when some men brought their wives for treatment. The lady would start to describe her symptoms, the husband would ask her to shut up and make statements like women had no sense and start on his version of her symptoms. There was a concerted social attempt to ensure that women were kept in their place. This attitude was carried to a ludicrous extent sometimes. To cite an example, some of the big old houses in Kerala have kitchen and pantry built a foot lower than the rest of the house. The purpose apparently was to keep the women who inhabited this area at a lower level as a symbol of their inferior status. This attitude to women was very similar to the treatment of lower castes in Kerala long ago. Kerala had a period in history when lower castes had to keep physical distance proportionate to their place in the caste hierarchy when they encountered a person of a superior caste in public space.

There was a surprising incident in my early days in Kolenchery. Entering the general ward one morning I saw a young woman struggling to breathe. A quick examination revealed the lady was in heart failure and needed immediate care. I practically ran around and made everyone hurry to administer medicines, start Oxygen and shift her into intensive care because I felt it was a matter of life and death. Investigation showed the heart failure was due to acute carditis as part of rheumatic fever. She recovered and was discharged. I received an anonymous letter a few days later castigating me for bossiness and unladylike behaviour that offended her. What I needed was a strong man to control me. A few days later I received another letter in the same handwriting and post office stamp abjectly begging me for documents necessary for an insurance claim, this time with a return address. Even in the dire circumstance, she could not deal with a woman doctor managing an emergency even though she was the beneficiary.

I had another very sobering experience while on rounds alone one Sunday. My senior at the time was a very charismatic and efficient male physician who was usually present on weekday rounds. When the sister and I entered the room for morning clinical rounds on this Sunday I saw the elderly male patient disappearing into the bathroom. The patient's wife was alone. We waited patiently. Time passed slowly. The sister and I looked at each other. The wife would not look at us or speak and I realised the man was hiding in the bathroom to avoid being examined by me, a female. I also remember a priest's wife asking me if I knew how to manage Rheumatic fever which her daughter was suffering from. Rheumatic fever is a condition even the most junior medical undergraduate knows all about. I just stared at her and the priest looked embarrassed. Another frequent sight that showed the general attitude of the populace towards women was when I entered a room for daily rounds in the wards. The patient's relative in attendance would sit comfortably in my presence and jump up with alacrity if a male assistant entered the room to the embarrassment of the junior and my amusement. (Getting up when a senior enters a room is considered a mark of respect). However, this attitude gradually changed except for rare instances. In fact, local people became protective and came to my rescue if I had problems inside or outside the hospital.

In MOSC I was fortunate to have broadminded male colleagues in the department of medicine throughout my working period. All of them brought remarkable skills to our department in addition to their clinical ability. The senior physician when I joined as a fresh MD was Dr Paul Puthuran, a bright and charismatic physician who became a role model for me. Dr C K Eapen who followed him had an inexhaustible fund of patience and capacity for hard work. Dr Regi Paul who worked with me for decades possesses great communication skills, Dr Abraham Ittyachen has exceptional organisational ability and Dr George Koshy is the most painstakingly conscientious doctor I have ever met. All of them have enriched my professional life.

A good proportion of internists in Kerala now are women. I do not know if they face discrimination because of their gender. If anyone does, I would advise her to acknowledge reality but always face it with dignity and confidence. Concentrate on personal growth, empathy and objectivity because the only person who can make you lesser is yourself.

CHAPTER 5

DOCTORS ARE HUMAN TOO

*I*nternal medicine often functions as the waste basket of medical practice. The relatively simple clinical problems are usually dealt with by the general practitioner. The diagnosed illnesses coming under the sub-specialities go to the specialists concerned. The unresolved puzzles belonging to no one are relegated to internal medicine. So, the physician functions mostly as a diagnostician looking for some elusive clue to enlighten him/her. Because of this, the internist has to have wide and fairly deep knowledge of every kind of illness and keep up with new developments to be effective. I think this fact partly accounts for newly qualified physicians rushing into subspecialties as soon as possible where they can focus on a narrower field. These fields may be more lucrative and prestigious too. But this phenomenon will eventually lead to too many specialists who are experts in one speciality and not enough internists who have wider and more comprehensive knowledge of people and diseases unless corrective steps are taken. I can vouch for the challenge of internal medicine.

Often the puzzles are common diseases having uncommon manifestations and like a criminal investigator, one has to look for missing clues. As a physician, I have had my share of these. I have succeeded sometimes and failed occasionally.

Some doctors consider clinical examination less important now as newer and more sophisticated investigations become widely available. For example, some cardiologists never carry a stethoscope and use only an echocardiogram to diagnose valve lesions of the heart. Newer facilities definitely improve diagnosis and management and complement clinical ability. But these facilities may not be available all the time at all the places. Some diseases are yet to have dependable diagnostic tests or the tests may be unaffordable for the average patient. Only clinical skills will aid the doctor in such situations. All doctors will agree that medicine is still an incomplete science and there are large lacunae in our understanding of the human body and the numerous diseases it is vulnerable to. Every generation of researchers adds new insights to this vast field and develops new tests, machines and medicines, but it is still far from perfect. The human eye is often capable of observing and reasoning out what laboratory tests and machines miss out. A day may come when sentient artificial intelligence can replace human doctors, but the day is still far away.

Recently I listened to a doctor who left medical practice in favour of Civil Service highlighting the reasons why the public resents and often attacks hospitals and staff. One of the reasons she cited was physically examining the patient and effectively communicating with them are no longer priorities for doctors. The result was an emotional disconnect between the patient and the doctor. An attitude of superiority and otherness makes patients and doctors antagonists. Newer equipments, investigations, medicines and treatment regimes certainly add to more precise diagnosis and cure, but doctors need to understand the importance of human emotions and physical examination. I have understood over the years that anxious patients find the doctor's touch comforting.

The inclusion of the medical profession under the Consumer Protection Act (CPA) has brought unanticipated problems for the treating doctor. The doctor's role is to promote healing. This can only be done if the doctor feels confident and the patient trusts the doctor. Mutual distrust is detrimental to the healing process and practice of medicine. Defensive medical practice has emerged out of the doctor's loss of confidence. He /she tries to avoid troublesome litigation by ordering investigations which may be very expensive and avoidable. Sometimes a treatable patient may be sent away to higher centres to avoid blame. A doctor needs survival skills and defensive medical practice is one way of surviving in the era of CPA. Legislation has to be sensitive to all these factors and make suitable modifications in the CPA for medical practitioners to eliminate tension between patient and doctor.

There can be no excuse for carelessness and negligence in medical practice because we are dealing with human lives. A doctor should be ethical and sincere in his/her dealings with patients. Effective communication and involving the patient and a responsible relative in decision-making is mandatory. It is important to identify the persons truly responsible and concerned about the patient and keep them informed about the patient's progress. A patient comes to the doctor or hospital in a very vulnerable state. All possible help should be given to him without monetary consideration or social status.

A clinician has to keep on updating his/her knowledge and skills. The patient's healing and welfare should be the foremost concern. Ego has no role in critical situations. One need not be reluctant to ask for a second opinion from a colleague, referring books or searching the internet when in doubt. Often voicing doubts aloud and speaking to a colleague makes difficult problems solvable.

Effective communication skills and capacity for empathy improve with practice, but initial training should start during undergraduate course in the medical college itself. The selection stage itself should include an assessment of the emotional quotient (EQ) of candidates. Clinical practice is stressful and involves a certain degree of self-sacrifice that often goes unappreciated by patients. It is easy for a clinician to feel dispirited and aggrieved. The ability to be objective while retaining sensitivity and empathy is a challenge, but it is essential to prevent early burnout of young doctors. Among all groups of professionals, medical doctors show the highest incidence of depression, suicide and early death. According to the Indian Journal of Psychiatry 30%of Indian doctors go through depression and 17% have considered ending their lives.

Society and patients too have obligations to a hardworking doctor. Equating an ill human being to a malfunctioning machine with totally predictable and easy-to-repair glitches is faulty. Illnesses do not affect everyone in a uniform manner. There are different manifestations of the same disease and these may change according to the time of consultation. The patient may fail to describe his symptoms correctly or may even hide some symptoms due to shame or ignorance. Then there are variables like age, heredity, health history, immunity, coexisting diseases, medications and following instructions correctly, etc. Response to treatment may vary due to unidentifiable reasons too. Despite the massive information load available on diseases the unknown intricacies of the human body and mind outweigh the known. Modern medicine has no panacea for all diseases. There are several diseases for which no cure has yet been discovered and doctors are not infallible. The patient should be made to understand these facts to the extent possible.

In rare situations, one may come across persons who revel in litigation, especially against doctors. Some are justifiable, but litigation based on facetious and false accusations adds unnecessary stress to a doctor's life. My team and I got into such a legal tangle unwittingly once.

A sixty-year-old lady was brought in semi-conscious state to the emergency department. She was a post office RD agent and was apparently well till the previous evening and had gone to bed at midnight after finishing all household chores. The husband went to wake her up at four am and could not wake her. She was taken to the local hospital which referred her to my hospital. Detailed examination did not reveal any physical abnormality. Metabolic workup was perfectly normal. A CT scan of the brain was also normal. We took blood and urine samples to check for poisons and drug overdose and kept her hydrated under observation.

The patient became more lucid the next morning and on repeated questioning said that she had taken three tablets before going to bed. Her son was on regular medication, so we asked the laboratory to check for these specific drugs. We went and spoke to the husband about what the patient said and about checking for drug overdose. This made the husband very angry and he immediately got the patient discharged and took her to another hospital forty-odd kilometres away.

A few weeks later we got an order from the Lokayukta to present ourselves before the judge on the patient's husband's complaint. The charges were medical negligence, insensitive careless nursing care and failure to diagnose intracranial bleeding from which the patient suffered. It took a lot of our time and effort to report for repeated hearings conducted at the court forty kilometres away. We requested for and obtained the medical records from the treating hospital. The records revealed that the second hospital had started the patient on treatment for meningitis and had done an MRI scan of brain four days after admission. The scan revealed an ischemic(deficient blood supply) stroke in the thalamic area. This could have happened any time during the intervening four days. Possible dehydration could have compromised an area with borderline blood supply leading to a small infarct. The CT scan done in our hospital was perfectly normal and close monitoring and a follow-up scan were what her condition required. We did not get the chance to observe the progression of her condition since she was taken away against medical advice because the husband was offended by her disclosure. The test for the specific drug done at a famous laboratory came back as strongly positive. Also it was possible that she took more than the three tablets she admitted to swallowing. It was lack of trust in us and taking offence at the suggestion of drug intake that resulted in this avoidable distress for all concerned. The case was dismissed. I was told the husband was a veteran litigant which may or may not be true because I have not seen him since to verify the matter.

A situation common to our society is even acquaintances who have no interest or stake in the patient's well-being visit them in the hospital as a social obligation and entertainment. They accentuate the patient's suffering and chances of superadded infection to a vulnerable patient. They may also make uncalled-for statements affecting the patient's morale and question the mode of treatment and cause general confusion. All doctors encounter such Job's comforters who provide uncalled-for consolation to the patient. I had such an experience some years ago. My husband developed oesophageal perforation and consequent infection of surrounding tissue(mediastinitis) after accidentally swallowing a small bone. He was in hospital for a month of intensive antibiotic treatment and eventually recovered. A group of acquaintances visited him in the hospital and tried to entertain him. One of them eloquently described with relish two similar cases he knew of. The tales ended with the statement that both patients died. The general public needs to be sensitised to the negative impact of their intrusive behaviour.

There is an enormous amount of research going on in Medical science with an equally massive amount of discoveries and inventions. These are of enormous benefit to the human race, but there is a downside to this progress. Some of the new inventions have actually made the doctor's job more complicated. One example is the confusion about the ethics of offering life support in some critical conditions. When a patient becomes too ill to sustain homeostasis (natural metabolic balance keeping all organs healthy and functioning) we resort to artificial life support to compensate for the failing organ system's function. Dialysis, mechanical ventilation, ECMO (Extracorporeal Membrane Oxygenation) are all examples. When the patient has a potentially curable disease and is otherwise healthy there is no confusion. Then it becomes a matter of all-out battle using all available means. But when the patient has incurable diseases or is very old what do we do? When there is sudden worsening and threat to the patient's life the doctor at hand has no time to consult with anyone, unless the deterioration was anticipated. Immediate resuscitation has to start when a patient goes into cardiac arrest. The doctor revives the patient and initiates expensive invasive life support like mechanical ventilation. When the progress is poor and recovery doubtful how do we decide to switch off the machines? The concerned relative has to deal with guilt if he requests termination of life support and faces a huge financial burden if it is continued. Sometimes poor families become destitute and homeless when a family member becomes critically ill and needs expensive invasive life support. So, this is a significant moral dilemma into which modern inventions have led the medical community and patient's caretakers. Where do we draw the line in invasive life support? Sometimes the patient has to suffer greater discomfort from interventions that will most likely not make him better. They are carried out because there are such options available and the doctor feels duty-bound to take advantage of the options and relatives feel guilty about denying them to the patient.

There is a legal process DNR (do not resuscitate) that can be executed when the patient is fully cognizant. But this is rarely done. So, the doctor and relatives are left in confusion. When I was a medical student we had a proactive senior professor in charge of radiation therapy. Their ward always had very ill cancer patients in great pain. When sudden cardiac arrest happened to one of them the duty doctor would immediately resuscitate the patient and continue with the required intravenous medications. When the professor was at hand he would put a stop to all the resuscitative activities going on and allow the patient to die. This may be deemed passive euthanasia which is a crime in India. This was fifty-five years ago and the professor passed away many years ago. I don't think any doctor would dare to stop life support on his own initiative in this age of litigation for medical negligence and the Consumer Protection Act.

Most of the patients who go to the hospital have a fair idea of what is wrong with them. The doctor only needs to listen to the story, examine the patient and decide on management. Then there are the cases unravelled by careful history taking and physical examination. Some cases need simple tests to confirm the diagnosis. A few cases like occult malignancies or uncommon autoimmune diseases require extensive and expensive investigations to arrive at accurate diagnosis. Treatment may be simple, complicated or unsuccessful according to the condition. Then there are the instances where only listening to the patient, examining him/her and following up any incongruity helps you solve the case. These are often common problems but with protean manifestations. Early intervention is usually simple, but delay may prove catastrophic in most cases. These are the truly rewarding experiences for the doctor to remember.

The incidents cited below are not exceptional. But they are problems that solved themselves on the strength of small incongruities noted and followed through. They did not need expensive investigations or brilliant elucidation. The cases and their management were relatively simple. But they were all potentially dangerous situations where expensive investigations would prove useless and delay catastrophic. Picking out incongruities and following them through saved the patient from greater expenses and suffering and the doctors from guilt, regret and possible litigation. Simple cases like these are the ones that gave me professional satisfaction and stay in my memory. The following are some instances I do remember.

A middle-aged lady was admitted with a recent increase in tiredness. She was found to have moderate anaemia that could explain her tiredness. During morning rounds we reassured her, started her on medicine for hookworms, iron and vitamins and wrote discharge. We proceeded to see the other patients, but a nagging doubt remained in my mind—why did she have a heart rate over hundred when she was at rest with a haemoglobin level of nine? She had no cardiac or thyroid disease. Was there an inapparent internal bleeding? So, we trooped back to the patient and questioned her about any symptom she missed telling us. She had a vague abdominal pain she did not tell us about because she often had such pain and it usually passed without any treatment. She was in her late forties and used to get only occasional periods. Examination of abdomen only elicited mild lower abdominal tenderness. An unlikely possibility of tubal pregnancy passed through our minds in spite of her age and negligible pain response. She was immediately sent for a sonogram of the abdomen that showed a large collection of blood in the pelvis. Emergency surgery was performed. She had a ruptured ectopic pregnancy and several pints of blood in the pelvis. The gynaecologist did an auto transfusion because the blood was fresh and the amount large. The patient's high pain threshold could have led to avoidable tragedy for her and distress for our medical team. Her age, irregular perimenopausal periods and high pain threshold had blindsided us.

A young college-going girl came to the outpatient clinic complaining of low back ache. She was otherwise well. I referred her to the orthopaedician who ordered X rays which were normal. He reassured her and prescribed pain killers. She came back to me a few days later with the same complaint. I thought of functional causes, reassured her and was going to send her away. As she was leaving I noticed her slightly tilted gait and asked her if she walked like that in college too. She assured me she indeed did because of pain. The thought that a pretty girl at that self-conscious young age would not want to make a spectacle of herself in college made me take her seriously. An MRI scan was ordered immediately and it revealed early tuberculosis of the spine.

A young person working as a nurse in a local hospital was admitted with swelling and redness of the whole of her left arm and a fever for two weeks. She had already had two courses of antibiotics from other hospitals and had no relief. We took an X-ray of the arm and were flummoxed to see several radiopaque patches and streaks on the X-ray. She stoutly denied having access to any radio-opaque dye or taking any injection at any time. During this time one of our sphygmomanometers (BP apparatus) fell and broke. As we collected the skittering mercury in a dish the thought struck me that this person was a nurse and had probably broken several BP apparatuses herself. She could have collected and kept the mercury. We questioned her again rather sternly. After initial denial, she confessed to injecting herself with liquid mercury collected from broken BP apparatuses and stored in her hospital. It was a poorly executed suicide attempt she was too ashamed to reveal. The surgeon had to make multiple incisions on her arm under general anaesthesia and scoop out several millilitres of liquid mercury. Fortunately, metallic mercury is inert and becomes toxic only after a chemical reaction. We assumed the residual mercury that could not be removed would slowly form toxic compounds in the tissues and so put her on low-dose chelation therapy for several weeks. The swelling slowly came down and she underwent expert counselling.

A lady in her sixties was brought unconscious with signs of severe organophosphate (OP) poisoning. The husband and son who brought her denied any chance of poisoning because they did not have any pesticide in the house and the patient never went out of the house. They were offended that we considered the possibility at all. This is often the reaction of relatives who bring poison victims to the hospital. The husband's reaction particularly was one of protesting too much. She was not fit to be shifted to another hospital so they kept her with us in spite of being offended by our questioning. We treated her as OP poisoning and she showed signs of improvement. The husband argued angrily with us every time he saw us. It was strange and suspicious behaviour and we had to inform the police as we suspected it to be a medico-legal problem.

When the patient was conscious and able to speak to us she denied taking any poison, she had only taken arishtam (herbal infusion) for rheumatism issued from the government Ayurvedic hospital near the husband's shop. It was brought by the husband and there was no seal on the bottle. The bottle was still with them. The son immediately went with the bottle to the ayurvedic doctor who had given the medicine and questioned him. The doctor assured him about the safety of the potion and to demonstrate this drank a large mouthful and became ill immediately. He was rushed to the local hospital which referred him to a city hospital at some distance. He was in intensive care for several weeks and later sent home in a bed-ridden condition. He passed away after years of suffering. The husband was prosecuted as the suspected poisoner. I do not know if he was sentenced or not, but the innocent doctor and his family suffered greatly. Being innocent and shrewd at the same time is hard, we can only try.

One morning a young bride was brought to the emergency department (ED) in a comatose state. She had no signs of infection, injury or poisoning. CT scan of the brain and metabolic workup proved normal. The relatives assured us she was perfectly active and happy the previous day. In fact, she had accompanied the church carol group that went singing from house to house the previous evening. We decided to keep her under observation on IV fluids and arranged for respiratory support if needed and got her blood checked for the presence of narcotics and moved on. The next patient was admitted with a non-poisonous snake bite. It dawned on us suddenly that carol singing was at night and the groups went on foot from house to house along ill-lit country lanes. The possibility of an unnoticed neurotoxic snake bite was probable. We went back to the patient and examined her feet. We could not find any definite bite marks but she had several small superficial wounds on both feet. Krait bites may be painless and the bite mark may go unnoticed. The poison is mainly neurotoxic and can result in paralysis, coma and death. There was no immediate diagnostic test available to confirm the suspicion. We called Dr Eapen who has great experience in snake bite management. He was kind enough to rush to the ED and give us moral support. We started the patient on anti-snake venom only based on our suspicion of krait bite as a therapeutic trial after obtaining the relative's consent. She became conscious in a few hours and was shifted to the ward for further treatment. She recovered fully in a few days.

It is astounding that the moderate-sized human animal with just 23 pairs of chromosomes has such complexity of cellular structure and function. In health, they all perform perfectly in the symphony of life with orderliness. It is also this complexity that makes the human body so vulnerable to loss of harmony and dysfunction. The vast number of diseases that result have varied manifestations in different individuals. Managing these varied diseases with incomplete knowledge makes medicine an art or an incomplete science at best. But knowledge is growing exponentially. Every doctor realises this as years pass and he/

she cannot remain complacent with what was learnt in medical schools. There are more diseases one is not aware of than the ones encountered in usual medical practice. My tryst with leptospirosis is proof of this dictum.

CHAPTER 6

RODENTS RUN OVER HUMANS!

Leptospirosis is not a new disease. It is a bacterial infection that spreads from animals like rodents to humans. It was first recognised in 1886 by Adolf Weil in Heidelberg, Germany. Later outbreaks of the disease were reported in the Andamans in the 1920s and 30s. For some reason, the Indian Medical Commission under the British made a categorical statement that leptospirosis was not a common disease on the mainland of India. I think this authoritative statement made the Indian medical community complacent enough to forget the disease. The disease disappeared from public and medical consciousness after 1930. There were short chapters on leptospirosis in Manson's text book of Tropical Medicine and other clinical textbooks, but no one took it as a disease relevant to late twentieth-century medical practice in India. Veterinarians however were aware of it as a cause of foetal loss in cattle.

Rodents Run Over Humans!

Welcome to Leptospires

Mr. George, the victim who inspired our study

During 1987 a number of young healthy males were admitted to our hospital from in and around Kolenchery with sudden onset of fever and body ache. Some recovered with symptomatic treatment, but several of them rapidly got sicker with bleeding tendency, breathing difficulty, shock and died suddenly. There was no diagnostic test available for any kind of haemorrhagic fevers in Kerala or surrounding states at the time. Our general tendency was to attribute it to "some unknown virus" and offer symptomatic treatment and genuine sympathy. Still, our team discussed different possibilities like yellow fever, Lassa fever, leptospirosis and even Ebola. We contacted different laboratories in the country none of which could help.

There was a local family that used to consult me if any of their members had medical problems because of their deep trust in me. The man of the house, Mr George was a recently retired government employee and a caring family man. He was admitted with a fever, low platelet count and bleeding tendency. Overnight his condition worsened and he died the same night. This upset me very much because I felt I failed the family and betrayed their trust. I felt compelled to make an all-out search to find the cause of this unidentified threat. Since leptospirosis was the only bacterial haemorrhagic fever under consideration and amenable to antibiotics we decided to give crystalline penicillin to patient with similar clinical spectrum which followed, on an empirical basis. Viral haemorrhagic fevers had no effective treatment at that time. (though now there are partially effective anti-viral drugs for a few viral infections like Lassa fever, and Hanta virus.) Meanwhile, all efforts to try and get a diagnosis would be made. I have to thank Dr C K Eapen and Dr Regi Paul, my colleagues, who gave me their staunch support.

We collected blood samples from patients who presented with similar symptoms –two samples a week apart if the patient survived and single samples from the ones who succumbed. Each sample was divided into three. When we had about two dozen samples I took one batch to Dr Jacob John (the well-known consultant virologist to WHO and paediatrician based in CMC) in Vellore and he promised to have the samples checked for haemorrhagic fevers like Dengue in laboratories outside India. Dr Grace Koshy, an eminent microbiologist and my teacher who was in MOSC at the time took particular interest and sent the second batch to Centre for Disease Control(CDC), Atlanta to check for antibodies against leptospires. One group we kept for any future investigation. Meanwhile, we found an old Leptospira culture procedure in a still older microbiology textbook that described how to prepare Fletcher medium to culture Leptospira. Dr Koshy agreed to try out the method and prepared special blood culture bottles and medium.

The next few weeks were of anxious waiting. Then the exciting results arrived from CDC and Dr John. Twenty-one of the twenty-four samples showed high levels of antibodies against Leptospira. All samples were negative for viral haemorrhagic fevers.

We had to wait longer for the culture results because Leptospires are slow-growing and take over weeks or months to grow in the culture medium we were using. Identifying Leptospires need a dark field microscope and we did not have one. None of us including Dr Koshy had ever seen Leptospires either. We found out that the veterinary institute at Mannuthy Agricultural College had a dark field microscope and their staff Doctor Chacko and Dr Radhakrihnan had done research on cattle leptospirosis. We contacted them and they agreed to look at our cultures if we could bring them to their laboratory. When we suspected Leptospira growth in the culture because of slight cloudiness in the test tubes after some weeks, Dr Koshy, Dr Regi Paul and the two technicians helping us Ms Sudha and Ms Annamma and I took the cultures to Mannuthy early morning. We were anxious and hopeful. Dr Chacko and Dr Radhakrishnan prepared smears of the cultures, looked under the dark field microscope smiled and invited us to look. There were thin bright thread-like organisms darting across the dark field. The thrill of that moment is unforgettable.

From then on we could treat leptospirosis with confidence and without hesitation because we had obtained convincing proof of the presence of human leptospirosis in our country side. We did a retrospective analysis of earlier cases with similar clinical profile and the antibody and blood culture positive cases. We noted and listed early clinical features and routine laboratory test results common to them. Based on these clinical and laboratory features we could identify leptospirosis in its early stage and initiate treatment before results of confirmatory tests became available. Diagnosis and treatment could be done with greater confidence early enough to prevent complications which usually occur when treatment is initiated late.

CHAPTER 7

WE ARE JUST THAT WAY!

We published our findings in The Transactions of the Royal College of Tropical Medicine and Hygiene. The article came out only in the June edition of 1990 but we had informed local hospitals and government agencies of our findings during the previous years. They were rather sceptical and looked at this as a publicity project for MOSC Hospital. There has always been an undercurrent of mistrust between the private and government health sectors in Kerala. Both look down on each other, but in actual functionality, they complement each other-a fact both often forget. When the local health authorities were informed of the presence of leptospirosis in the area there was only scepticism and no positive action officially to confirm or disprove our report.

Inquiries however came from abroad about leptospirosis and our publication in 1990. One was from Dr Chris Everard a UK citizen who had worked on Leptospirosis in Barbados, West Indies. He came to Kolenchery to see our work and the rural areas from where the patients came. He was also kind enough to supply us with a non-pathogenic Patoc1 strain of Leptospires to prepare the antigen for ELISA* test for laboratory diagnosis of leptospirosis. Dr Koshy had left MOSC by this time and there was no qualified microbiologist to organise and supervise further study. So, I had to step in with my undergraduate level of knowledge in microbiology. The technicians Ms Sudha and Annamma were able and gave me their full support in our tentative efforts to produce a reliable antigen for the standard ELISA test because commercial test kits were not available in India at the time. We were able to establish this test in MOSC by trial and error by 1991.

Dr Everard had given us some antigen preparation to do a simple slide test for quick Leptospira antibody screening without quantification. We used this antigen to do a comparative study of leptospiral antibody presence in the local farming population and student volunteers unexposed to farm work. Most of the farm workers tested positive for leptospiral antibodies while 95% of the students who were hostel inmates were antibody negative. We published the results in the Kerala Medical Journal in April '94. After these developments, the medical community came to terms with the widespread prevalence of leptospirosis in the wet farming areas of Kerala. Gradually it was recognised and highlighted at the national level by both private and government sectors. It was sad that Western validation was necessary for the medical fraternity to accept and trust this geographically relevant findings reported by locals like us.

Later we came across the same resistance to accepting data from private or mission hospitals when MOSC started reporting cases

---

ELISA - Enzyme Linked Immuno-Sorbent Assay

of Dengue fever in and around Kolenchery in 2000. Over the years outbreaks of Dengue have become common during and immediately following monsoons and localised epidemics of Dengue are reported in Kerala annually. In 2016 the burden of dengue was so high in Kolenchery that we had to convert a large auditorium into a patient ward to accommodate the rising number of cases. I think the same denial is being repeated in the case of Hepatitis B outbreaks that happen in the state sporadically.

A small field study we undertook in one locality in 2016 showed the wide presence of blood-sucking deerflies in the area. These flies usually feed on cattle and can cause anaemia in them because of the significant amount of blood they suck. They also bite humans and when disturbed while feeding flit from one host to another making mechanical transmission of the virus possible. We raised the possibility of mechanical transmission of hepatitis B virus from human carriers by this process in a scientific article and suggested further studies. The only response we found was an academic analysis of obscure data to deny the possibility and no attempt to do a field study. What is needed is for researchers to go out into the affected areas, trap the flies from affected localities and do scientific studies to prove or disprove the possibility.

Clinical presentation of leptospirosis was severe and catastrophic in the 80s and 90s because the population was unexposed to the organism and lacked herd immunity. Late diagnosis compounded the problem. Now leptospirosis is endemic in Kerala and there is some level of protective antibody in most farming populations. Awareness of the public and medical communities also helps in early detection and treatment making it less fearsome now.

I often wondered why a long-forgotten bacterial infection made such a dramatic re-entry into this community. Chatting with a local farmer gave me a probable clue. The Periyar Valley irrigation project was commissioned to facilitate more intense cultivation in this area in the 1976–77 period. Prior to this rice fields were cultivated once a year and left fallow to dry out in summer till the rains came. With the new irrigation facility year-round rice and pineapple cultivation became possible and soil remained moist throughout the year. Continuous cultivation of rice and pineapple made food available for rodents all year round. This plenty enabled the rodent population to multiply gradually over the next few years. The small waterbodies around and constant moisture in the soil helped Leptospires survive and spread because Leptospires excreted in rodent urine remain viable for weeks or months in moist soil and stagnant water. Contact with this contaminated soil and water during work or leisure activities leads to human infections. The emergence of leptospirosis may be called an unavoidable and direct effect of our green revolution.

Kerala is densely populated and is also getting rapidly urbanised. The wet and humid climate along with improper waste disposal add to the possibility of newer infectious and environmental diseases appearing or reemerging. Better modes of waste disposal, public awareness and proactive administrative interventions are essential to prevent environmental degradation adding to our existing challenges and bringing in new diseases. But urging the slow-moving administrative machinery to improve the waste disposal method is like butting one's head against a stone wall. The public's lack of civic sense is equally responsible for this state.

The institution and our medical team are truly indebted to the heroes who came to our help at appropriate times—Dr Grace Koshy, Dr Jacob John, Dr Chris Everard, Dr Radhakrihnan and Dr Chacko of Veterinary College Mannuthy, The Royal Tropical Institute, Amsterdam, Leptospira reference centre, Hereford and CDC, Atlanta -all of them helped us in containing this life and death problem. I especially remember Hans who identified all our serovars in Amsterdam including a new serovar cultured from our patient Bharathy and named it after her. Sadly, Hans passed away shortly after this while dancing in a nightclub.

Dr Everard put us in touch with Dr Terpstra, head of biomedical research laboratory of The Royal Tropical Institute, Amsterdam and Leptospira laboratory at Leptospira Reference Laboratory, Hereford, UK.I was invited to undergo a short observer training programme to learn diagnostic techniques for leptospirosis in both places. I was able to do this in March -April 1997, almost a decade after leptospirosis made its appearance in Kolenchery. After short stints in these laboratories, we were able to establish a Leptospira laboratory in MOSC with a modest WHO grant. Now standard ELISA test kits to diagnose leptospirosis are available commercially. Topics on leptospirosis form the major themes our PG students choose for thesis work. The government sector has listed leptospirosis as a major health risk to the agrarian communities in spite of the initial scepticism.

However, this will not be the end of the story. Newer diseases continue to emerge and most are zoonotic–i.e. natural hosts are animals, but can affect humans due to contact with host animals or human intrusion into the host animal's habitats. Nipah,

Hantavirus diseases Marburg virus, scrub typhus are all examples. Human encroachment into natural habitats of animals and environmental changes cause the emergence or reappearance of these diseases. Pathogens lurking in hitherto unidentified sources or as bioweapons in laboratories can push the human race into tragic epidemics. A recent example is how human interference triggered the calamitous covid 19 pandemic that is still doing the rounds around the globe. Hopefully nations will be more circumspect in the future in interfering with nature in general and pathogens in particular. Our own leptospirosis story is a reminder of how the fine equilibrium in nature is disturbed by unavoidable developmental activities for human needs. It also reminds me of our psychological need for Western validation before trusting our own work.

India's healthcare system consists of both the government sector and private sector almost in equal proportion. As mentioned earlier there is an unspoken area of conflict between the two. I witnessed and experienced the wariness each sector harbours about the other when there was a large influx of retired government medical college teachers into MOSC when it transformed into a medical college. For persons like me who put patient welfare above official protocols and seniority, a few of these senior doctors seemed obsessed with protocols and keeping subordinates as a compliant labour force sans initiative. Some of them generally discouraged original thinking and personal initiative. They also seemed to consider doctors in the non-governmental sector charlatans.

Doctors in the government sector begin their career as academically very competent, but some of them become complacent because of government support and job security. Doctors in the private sector on the other hand have to keep up with newer developments and have to develop good communication skills to be successful–a fact often forgotten. Many doctors do not enter government service for fear of corruption, political interference and possible vendetta. I think there is always scope for constant improvement in both sectors and they should complement each other. In place of mutual wariness, the two sectors should liaise to provide better and affordable service to patients and promote research to find solutions for difficult health problems prevalent in their areas. This is a message I wish to give the government health department, private health sector and doctors alike and I hope they will lend an ear to it.

There is a long-established custom in CMC of a grand farewell party being given to undergraduates who complete their training and leave the student hostels. On these solemn occasions, the departing students are expected to give verbal gifts and advice to their juniors. Likewise, if I am asked today at the tail end of my professional practice to give advice to prospective doctors waiting with great expectations to enter a glamorous profession, I say do not be deceived, there is no glamour in this profession. You will be entering a world of pain and suffering. If you are expecting great wealth there are better ways of acquiring it like starting a business or pharmaceutical company or manufacturing diagnostic equipment and materials. As a committed doctor who believes in ethical practice you can make a decent living because as Jesus said a worker deserves his wages, but you will never be affluent. If you expect a stress-free life with grateful clientele again you will be disappointed -even your best effort sometimes may not result in healing the patient and even if it happens the patient may not appreciate you. If you can accept lifelong learning and daily stress as part of the job and get satisfaction from doing your best you are clinician material. If not choose a paramedical or preclinical field where you do not have to directly interact with a lot of unhappy people. However, sometimes fortunate clinicians come across patients who are genuinely grateful and actually pray for their wellbeing.

CHAPTER 8

COLONIALISM HAUNTS US

I was born in the early post-independence era. We lived in a small village where everyone I knew was literate, but highly educated people were few. Most families were happy if their children got through SSLC and went for job-oriented training. Teaching, clerical jobs, nursing and defence services were the job providers. But I remember how people were hungry for national and international news. They eagerly waited for the daily newspaper to read the news. Malayala Manorama was the most popular daily and their weekly magazine was equally popular. People used to sit around and discuss daily news and even the serial stories in the weekly. The cartoon serial Boban and Molly were the favourite of children and adults alike. Somehow this group of rural folk including my family was infused with patriotic fervour regardless of caste or creed. We children also felt we had to do our best to improve the stature of our newly independent nation. We were taught to revere "Bharat Matha" and emulate freedom fighters. Gandhiji, Nehru, Vinobha Bhave and Subhash Chandra Bose were our heroes. Sarojini Naidu was a familiar name. In fact, all of us harboured some anti-British feelings even though a few years had passed after independence. The shared emotion of national pride was uniform among ordinary rural folks like us regardless of caste, creed or social status and the feeling has stayed with me all through.

As I came in contact with more affluent and sophisticated Indians in the medical profession, I felt that most of them were secretly ashamed of their country and wanted to move west as soon as possible. Most of them admired America and Britain more than India with its unsophisticated population. National pride was for the less privileged. Even as I write this there is an exodus of youngsters to the West as students and job seekers from all over India. This emigration is not driven by civil unrest, religious persecution or abject poverty which are the usual reasons for human migration. Even youngsters from well-to-do families are making a beeline to emigrate to UK, USA and Australia. Some of them spend large sums of money to emigrate illegally and earn humiliation for themselves and the country. They could have built their own enterprises in this country with the money wasted on unethical agents. Obviously, we have failed to inculcate a sense of national pride in this generation and they retain some of the sense of inferiority their ancestors suffered in colonial India. Part of the blame belongs also to the successive governments that fail to generate job opportunities for the youth. On the other hand, if globalisation and electronic media have made our youngsters perceive the world in global terms and not in terms of nations this trend may be a positive one. If so the future of humanity becomes brighter with a more tolerant and united world with less strife and wars. In the distant future national barriers may come down and humanity may become one great family. Such are our improbable dreams.

One byproduct of the mass migration of youngsters is that they leave behind "orphaned" parents who find refuge in retirement homes which are mushrooming in Kerala. Those who cannot afford this arrangement end up at the mercy of poorly maintained government orphanages. Culturally, Indian parents invest all their emotional and material resources on their children and these children are dependent on their parents even after reaching adulthood unlike in Western culture which promotes self-reliance and individual autonomy. The young generation of Indians finding their own destiny is admirable, but many of them are not enlightened enough to work and finance their own education and migration. Many parents become destitute by spending all their savings and selling homes to finance foreign education and the emigration of their children. I know parents who have mortgaged their homes to send their children abroad for studies and are reduced to a hand-to-mouth existence. Foreign aspirations of these youth, at least in some cases, seem to be a new avatar of the declining though still prevalent dowry system that used to impoverish underprivileged families when daughters were married off.

There were sixty students in my MBBS batch. CMC provides highly subsidised education. (Even my brother George who was not rich could see me through medical college while bringing up a family of three on a stringent budget.) All except a dozen of my classmates left India for Western countries immediately after MBBS. A few stayed back to do PG courses and some of them too moved west later permanently. I once asked one of my PG batch mates preparing to move to UK why he wanted to live in a foreign country as a second-class citizen. His shocking reply was that it was better to live in a first-class country as a second-class citizen than a first-class citizen in a third-class country.

It does not surprise if a people, after two hundred years of colonial rule that disempowered them and trivialised their ancient culture, lost self-confidence and pride in their own heritage. All of us suffer from this lack of confidence to varying degrees. But the more educated and privileged groups need to have more insight and a sense of duty to realise that it is up to them to work for a resurgent and confident India. Instead of rushing abroad to partake of the affluence and comforts built up by the former colonial countries that looted India's wealth, it is up to us to lift up our own country. I can easily identify with the disadvantaged sections and those struggling to make a living or trying to improve skills by going abroad or settling there. But people who benefitted from our subsidised education system and belong to the privileged groups need to pay back the country in proportion either financially or in terms of service.

Unfortunately, even politicians who should be setting examples in national pride and nation building seem to be under the sway of colonialism still. We see some of them rushing to foreign countries for treatment of ordinary illnesses at public expense. This is when we have excellent medical institutions in this country with doctors totally capable in their fields. The powerful seem to think that what treatment ordinary Indians are happy to receive is not good enough for them and that treatment in

Western countries is superior. It is true that there is more research going on in the West to unravel the unknown and to find newer drugs. But there are excellent centres throughout India that score over Western ones in speedy patient care, efficiency in carrying out established management protocols and cost-effective treatment. Paramedical staff working in UK, USA and Australia often come to us for treatment because they have more faith in our system for routine medical care. Those in power too should respect our people and institutions and strive to build them up. Our society itself needs to break free of its mental colonisation which is a reality. Psychological freedom is more difficult to attain than administrative freedom. It may take Indians another two hundred years to become completely confident.

I witnessed a strange scene in the YWCA canteen in Chennai some years ago. Our family was on a sightseeing tour of Chennai and were staying in the YWCA guest house. One morning we went to their canteen for breakfast and waited patiently for a waiter to approach our table to take orders. Two waiters loitering around, seemingly unaware of customers were not approaching any table to take orders. A group of Indian academics staying at the place entered the hall carrying papers and books obviously on the way to a conference. They were in a hurry and tried to attract the attention of the waiters who ignored their urgent signals. Then an elderly white man entered the room and the electrified waiters both rushed to him, found a table and were all attention. One thin old Indian lady of the academic group carrying a book titled' Magic of Sprouted Grains' was so outraged that she yelled at the waiters. How can we accuse the whites of racism when we still have not overcome racism and casteism? The affluent imitate Western attire and accents and feel superior. The poor still view the white man as Sahib (master or owner).

In 1997 Dr Dhani Ram Barua, a cardiac surgeon in Guwahati, India, transplanted a pig heart in his patient Purno Saikia who was terminally ill from heart failure as a last-ditch effort to save his life. The heart functioned for a week but was rejected and patient Saikia passed away ten days after the transplant. A ten-day survival was fair for this first attempt. The mainstream media caused a furore which probably induced the government to jail the doctor. Dr Barua's institute was burnt down. The doctor who should only have been taken to task and reprimanded was jailed for forty days and vilified in the media. Instead, he could have been encouraged to be totally accountable and transparent in his research and provided facilities for finetuning his research to find effective methods of tissue matching and possible antigenic modification of porcine tissue. Pig organ systems have 80% similarity with human models. Antigenically porcine tissue has fewer dissimilarities from human tissue and hence lower probability of transplant rejection among all inter-species organ transplantation.

It was evident that Dr Barua's patient could not have been expected to survive long. At worst, the doctor's attempt was a daring and original experiment in a hopeless situation. But subsequent events and the treatment meted out to Dr Barua must have nipped Indian biomedical researchers' enthusiasm for original research in the bud. When porcine heart xenotransplantation was repeated twenty-five years later in Maryland USA in January 2023 it was celebrated as a historic event all over the world including in the Indian media unquestioningly. Our media, still suffering from colonial hangover, wait for validation from the West even in matters of national interest instead of backing local enterprise and research. With all the expensive studies and research done in the long twenty-six intervening years in the USA the patient David Bennet died two months later.

Now Indian scientists may join the bandwagon of research on xenotransplantation. After all, some of the biomedical of research in Indian medical institutions are duplications of Western projects. Research in India ought to be tailored to find solutions to problems particular to our land and should have practical application. Western researchers are likely to focus on Western health concerns like genetic abnormalities, degenerative diseases and neoplastic diseases. Our special problems like nutritional deficiencies, infectious diseases, local environmental problems are not priorities for the West but should be our concern.

A glaring example of our failure to deal with regionally relevant health problems is the manufacture of antivenom to treat poisonous snake bites. More than a hundred years ago the British managed to capture the Indian subcontinent's four most deadly species of venomous snakes from the Madras residency, extract their venom and produce a crude antivenom. The venoms were injected into horses and sheep which produced antibodies to them. The animals were bled and antibodies harvested from their plasma. This antivenom preparation contained components of animal serum other than the essential antibodies to the venoms and could cause severe allergic reactions in humans.

Seventy-seven years after independence India still depends on the same antivenom manufacturing method that hopefully employs better purifying techniques. Dangerous allergic reactions are still very common. But the astonishing fact is that India has about sixty species of poisonous snakes and the country accounts for half of all annual deaths due to snake bites globally. But we still manufacture the same quadrivalent antivenom that has no effect against any of the other species of venomous snakes. Northern India has different poisonous snakes for which no antivenom is produced. In southwest India a very poisonous species, the hump-nosed pit viper(Hypnale Hypnale) causes death and morbidity in the villages, but there is no effective antivenom available for hypnale envenomation.

Research and serious efforts to produce effective antivenom for at least the more poisonous ones among the fifty-seven forgotten poisonous snakes in India do not seem to be a priority for big biotechnology and pharma giants. I often feel that patriotic Indians who want to solve India's problems and see India rise gravitate to space research and defence services while the biotechnology sector and pharma segments seem to be targeting maximum profit for minimum research. It is not talent that is lacking, but the will (political?) to face challenges. Indian scientists have proven to be great problem solvers whenever they have taken up a cause earnestly.

Many of the distinguished doctors and nurses in USA and UK are people who got their basic degrees in India. They form a significant part of the brain drain India faces. Many Scientists and business people who should have been the moving force of our country's development chose these countries. Why?

One reason as mentioned above is our failure to give our children the sense of pride, optimism and desire to work for India's upliftment. Financial difficulties and inadequate job opportunities are also factors. The ruling class is often the cause of driving away brilliant young people by lack of encouragement, appreciation and red-tapism in the government machinery. Nepotism and corruption in power politics give rise to disenchantment in the youth.

Reservation policy without encouraging excellence has played a part too. It is often the creamy layer of a community that benefits from blanket reservation. Children from disadvantaged sections in these communities who are ignorant about government policies are left out. These children should be given accommodation, good nutrition and special coaching in good schools free of cost. This would enable them to realize their potential and compete with other children for higher education and jobs. This will lead to improvement in our educational standard and consequent excellence in our nation's all-round development. The most important gift the nation can give its disadvantaged youth is a level playing field for opportunities, self-confidence and optimism about the future rather than widely resented reservation.

The present Indian attitude to the country's long colonisation is interesting. A significant number of Indians are ambivalent about this. A few are even delusional and nostalgic about how the philanthropic British established railways, schools and hospitals for the natives and we are able to build on the foundation laid by them. There is only a very small grain of truth in this.

The defenders of the Raj, both British and Indian, actually believed if India had not been colonised it would still be in the dark ages. This opinion comes from only a minority of Indians who actually benefited from low to medium-level jobs and favours under the British. The vast majority of Indians suffered greatly rather than benefited from colonial rule. The minority that helped the British to run the colonial ruling machine got rewarded. They forget that the defining intent of all colonisation is exploitation. The modest infrastructure the British built in India was aimed at their comfortable travel in this vast country and to facilitate transport of its natural resources to Britain. India would have developed in a different manner with a more self-confident population if colonisation had not happened. The most significant side effect of colonisation was the loss of self-confidence and national pride of the people. Every Indian should read Shashi Tharoor's book on the British Raj-Not to take revenge, but to learn from history.

The role of Christian missionaries in India often evokes contradictory emotions among Indians now. What cannot be denied is that some Christian missionaries from various Western countries and a few philanthropic Westerners were instrumental in empowering Indians by introducing modern education in the country. The British rulers did not oppose missionary activity because educational institutions helped to train local talent to help them in running their ruling machinery. They needed literate Indians in subordinate positions in the army and administrative services and probably did not anticipate the empowerment that would result from modern education. The emergence of educated and enlightened Indians inspired and enabled the masses to unite in their demand for India's freedom. India was also able to eradicate evil practices like Sati through the active intervention of enlightened Indians with support from the empathetic ones among the Westerners. In spite of some proselytising, most missionaries had good intentions and were the silver lining to the very dark cloud of colonialism.

It is remarkable in itself that a millennium of invasions, internecine conflicts and two hundred years of colonisation did not wipe out a culture and people as they did elsewhere. We escaped the fate of the indigenous people of America, Australia or New Zealand in spite of years of degradation, apartheid and cruelty. The argument that our survival was because the invaders and colonisers were benign rulers is not tenable. If they were so benign the indigenous people and cultures of America, New Zealand, Arabia and Australia could not have been decimated. The East India Company and the British Raj were successful in subjugating and degrading India and its people taking advantage of intrigues, jealousy, treachery and in fights among the rulers of the numerous kingdoms. But they were unable to destroy the social fabric of ordinary Indian people with deep-rooted traditions. Despite all its faults, Indian civilisation survived mainly because of the pre-existing social structure, diversity of the country and resilience of ordinary people. Also ruling the subcontinent must have been like attacking five hundred different countries and trying to keep control over them all. The Indian ability to assimilate outside customs and ideas may also have assisted this saga of self-preservation of the ancient civilisation. As for the British their immediate reason to leave India must have been the post war financial crisis in Britain and wide spread participation of all strata of Indian society in the freedom struggle.

My mother used to tell us stories of how during the world war the local government officials used to arrive at her father's house when rice harvesting started. They would confiscate the major portion of harvested rice without intimation or any payment. Families which used to produce surplus rice were reduced to starvation level and subsisted on available farm products like tapioca and jack fruit. I remember the general poverty of ordinary people in the 50s and the 60s in my own childhood. India's growth in the two hundred years of colonialism was negative. Now I marvel at the comparative prosperity achieved in Kerala and India as a whole in the last few decade in my own lifetime in spite of our large population. Still there are pockets of abject poverty and exploitation especially among the tribal and rural population. The Western print and visual media both continue to highlight and exaggerate post-independent India's deficiencies and seem ignorant of the vast positive changes that have happened here in just seventy odd years—a rather short period in the history of a nation. Both facts need to be acknowledged. There are disparities and injustice still, but I am optimistic about the future of India. We have a lot of catching up to do for the centuries of lost developments and emancipation of minds. There is no shame in receiving know-how and help from other countries in areas where we are deficient as a nation, but our ultimate aim should be self-sufficiency in all fields including technology, innovation, research and happiness of the people.

CHAPTER 9

EUROPEAN VENTURE

When I had the opportunity for a short training in Leptospira laboratory methods my institution gave me a subsistence allowance for two months study visit in Europe. I had not gone outside India and this prospect made me nervous. Still, I decided to take the chance anyway. So, entrusting the care of my two children to my husband and a helper I began my tour. I thought of the enterprise shown by the pioneering Malayalee nurses with no experience of travel setting forth to all corners of the world. My courage and initiative should be at least equal to theirs. So, on 16th April '97, I set out from Chennai airport on a British Airways flight which took eight hours to reach Heathrow airport. I do not remember the details of the flight except I was dozing off frequently. The passenger next to me was a pretty white girl travelling alone. The teenager was asking for and swilling wine repeatedly. She also asked me for the candy the hostess had supplied me with. I also remember a supercilious white male steward trying to chat with me as we were disembarking. Other than that, the flight was uneventful. I had a Schengen visa and had to complete immigration procedures at Heathrow airport before taking the connecting flight to Schiphol Airport, Amsterdam.

The immigration counter was something else. There were separate queues for whites and coloured people. The whole place was grey and gloomy matching my mood. The counter was staffed by a white woman. Helping her apparently to keep order was a plump dark woman (obviously of Indian origin.)in a blue saree. This lady seemed to be in a very bad temper and kept hectoring the coloured queue. Her special target was a young turbaned Sardarji whom she kept shouting at in a mixture of ungrammatical Hindi and English. The white woman seemed placid and unhurried, taking no notice of the scene. Maybe the saree lady was ordered to be rude and abusive to Indians as a reminder of their days of subjugation. I wondered why so many Indians wanted to enter such an unfriendly country and had to remind myself I had come to their country for a specific purpose and the other Indians too had equally legitimate reasons to put up with this treatment.

I had about an hour to wait for the Amsterdam flight which I spent watching my fellow passengers. I remember seeing a very Malayalee-looking orthodox Bishop in the usual regalia also waiting alone. When the short flight landed at Schiphol it was already dusk. To my relief, there was a person holding a placard with my name at the exit. This was Dr Rudi, deputed by the Royal Tropical Institute (RTI) to receive me and take me to my hotel. It was the tail end of winter and still cold and dreary. The trees were all bare and I thought they had somehow got burnt. Dr Rudi assured me they would all be blooming by the end of the month. He took me to a medium-range hotel and left me at the reception after giving me directions about reaching the RTI the next day. The daily charge for a single room was a hundred dollars. All I had with me was a thousand dollars in traveller's cheques to tide over two months and I was wondering how this was possible. Anyway, I couldn't stand and wonder in the foyer all night since I was in jet lag and feeling very sleepy. So, I paid and took the key to the room which was matchbox sized with enough room for a bed and a small attached bathroom. I only remember locking the door and lying on the bed to instantly fall asleep.

Fourteen hours later loud repeated knocks at the door woke me up. It was late morning. The room boy informed me that a priest and his wife were waiting at the reception for me. I am not an ardent church-going Christian, but before setting out for Europe I had visited Father Adai of the Jacobite Syrian Church to inform him of my trip and asking for advice about preparing for the trip. He was a seasoned traveller all around the globe including Europe. The kind priest had informed his friends in Amsterdam of my visit. The Syrian priest and his lovely wife had come to invite me to stay with them at Father Adai's request. Considering my depleting resources I gratefully accepted their invitation. (Pragmatism took precedence over pride). I have some difference of opinion with the church about their dogmas and love of money and power, but it has to be conceded they have the great ability to network and give help to its members if they want. I hoped to get some inexpensive lodgings near the institute later.

The Syrian priest and wife lived in a one-bedroom flat in one of the old stately apartment complexes on the banks of canals linked to river Amstel. These buildings date back before the World War but are still in good repair. I was reminded of the pictures of the house where Anne Frank lived while in hiding. I did not have the opportunity to go searching for it. The couple was kind enough to offer me their living room sofa, breakfast and dinner. The situation was not disagreeable, but I was constrained to intrude into the tiny living space of the young couple who were very kind to me. I am not used to a luxurious life, but am used to spacious living areas. Fortunately, again their friend Navroz, a Syrian girl doing a sociology undergraduate course at Amsterdam University was a paying guest in the upstairs bedroom of a lady Presbyterian minister. There was a spare bedroom there that I could occupy free of cost for the whole of my twenty-three days stay in Amsterdam. Naturally, I accepted the offer with alacrity. The house was in Amstelveen, a suburb of Amsterdam. I could walk to the local metro station and travel by the metro in twenty minutes to and fro the institute at a nominal fare.

Amsterdam is a truly cosmopolitan city. I did not foray into the city centre often, but what I saw was impressive. It looked like a dignified and friendly city. People in general seemed relaxed. There was no reluctance to smile and reply if I asked for help or direction. Throughout my three-week stay, I only came across one incident of probable racism. The Institute had several canteens. In one of them, one waiter kept serving the white customers who came after me and pretended not to see me. I moved on to another canteen which served me promptly according to order.

Study Tour

There was an impressive mix of different nationalities in Amsterdam and practically everyone spoke some English willingly. Immigrants of Middle Eastern appearance were present everywhere, mostly from Turkey and Syria. I was told they, along with the Surinamese immigrants, were the major workforce in construction and cleaning jobs very much like the workers from Assam and Bengal in Kerala now. We hold dignity of labour as an ideal, but do not practice it where physical labour is concerned. This seemed to be the reality even in Europe.

In over three weeks of stay, I did not come across any unfriendly experience in Holland. People were busy but the city as such was not crowded. Like all cities, there must be an underbelly to this city too where squalor, crime, prostitution, drug deals and fear lurked, but I had no reason to venture there. I heard of them from

Navroz. My exposure to the city was the daily metro travel and the few occasions I was taken to some parts of it by my friends. They were all pleasant experiences.

My itinerary included a two-week visiting observer stint at the diabetic centre in the German town of Bad Oeynhausen. The contrast between Amsterdam and Bad Oeynhausen was striking. In Amsterdam, the staff in general had some knowledge of the rest of the world and willingly spoke English. Some of the doctors and medical students I met had visited parts of India including Kerala. I must confess to being embarrassed when some of them recollected the intrusive stares of men they encountered in Kerala. Apart from this, my stay in Amsterdam was fruitful and satisfying.

The staff at the Royal Tropical Institute were always willing and helpful. It was a busy place with enthusiastic doctors, staff and researchers. Their laboratory was a hive of activity testing samples from the whole of Holland. With its dykes and low-lying moist agricultural land leptospirosis is an occupational hazard for its farmers. Apparently, Cuba also has a major problem with leptospirosis. The Cuban government had deputed a senior technician for training in laboratory diagnostic techniques for leptospirosis to the RTI. She was overwhelmed by Amsterdam. The first thing she did on arrival was to dye her hair blonde and find some Cuban compatriots in the city and become a busy tourist. The department was hard pressed to find her whereabouts to train her. I saw her on a few occasions when she paid flying visits to the institute. She said she had shifted to the house where her compatriots lived and had become their unofficial cook and house keeper. I often wonder what happened to her.

Dr Terpstra, Rudi, Hanah, Mareena, Hans, and Roeselyn were all busy, but always ready to clarify any doubts I had and give advice. I could get all the cultures and sera samples I had brought with me identified and serotyped. I returned with enough know-how and materials to establish MAT (Microscopic Agglutination Test) in our laboratory in MOSC. MAT though cumbersome, is still the gold standard in serological diagnosis of leptospirosis. This was very useful in our ten-year-long field study of leptospirosis in the rural areas around Kolenchery which was published in the Indian Journal of Medical Research in 2008. MOSC produced the first PhD holder in human leptospiral study in India when Dr Sheila Sugathan received her doctoral degree in leptospirosis from Mahatma Gandhi University. She carried out the MAT in over a thousand sera samples collected in our ten-year field study.

I remember a small incident when Dr Terpstra and his wife later visited MOSC hospital and I took them for lunch in our hospital staff canteen. Mrs Terpstra asked me repeatedly if the hospital was feeding the staff subsidised lunch because they were starving. She had only good intentions, but had the notion that India was so poor that most Indians were starving. I had to assure her repeatedly that most people she saw there could afford their basic needs of food, shelter and clothing without much difficulty. Somehow Europeans still cannot get around the idea of the starving millions of India even now. Western media's obsession with India's universal poverty and biased reportage must be the reason for this belief. She also commented on the heaped rice on the plates people were taking to their seats at the tables. The emotional connection Malayalees have with rice is well known, but we do eat too much rice.

Hans was the main person instrumental in testing all our samples from Kolenchery. He identified a new serovar (serovariety) in one culture isolated from our patient Bharathy. It was aptly named Serovar Bharathy. I also remember Hans taking me to see a smaller laboratory to show how it functioned. I was sad to learn later how he was stabbed in a club in Amsterdam and after recovery dropped dead while dancing.

Several pleasant memories come to mind when I think of Amsterdam. I visited my original hostess a few times and we used to walk along the canal in front of her apartment. Once we were reprimanded by a passing boatsman who saw us feeding the ducks in the canals. He told us we were actually feeding the rats and helping them to multiply. I was in agreement because leptospirosis surfaced in Kolenchery due to increased food availability for rodents resulting in their population explosion.

One bus ride with Navroz made me aware of the reach of the Indian diaspora. The driver who managed the fare also was a short dark plump Tamilian who was delighted to see another Indian. He refused to let us pay our fare for the ride. I wonder if he paid it from his own pocket. I enjoyed the daily walks to and fro the Amstelveen metro station and my place of stay too. The road was practically deserted except for the occasional car, pedestrians or lone cyclists and was lined by cherry trees. It was wonderful to see the trees which looked almost dead when I arrived suddenly blooming and covered in pink and purple flowers by my departure time.

One particular solo bus trip that alarmed me at first turned out memorable. I boarded a bus from the Institute to visit the priest and his wife. The bus manned only by the driver was supposed to stop where they lived. The driver forgot to stop the bus for me to get off. When both of us realised this he reassured me saying the return trip passed by the same stop and I could get a quick glimpse of the city and surroundings free of cost before being dropped off. So, I had a pleasant ride and had glimpses of river Amstel with classic stately buildings along its banks, small wooden houses standing on wooden stilts in water and unending fields of tulips and lilies grown commercially. I was reminded of the many Hindi movie songs on Doordarshan in which these flower fields played the backdrop.

Floriculture as we know is a major occupation bringing in large income to Holland, Kokenhauf being its major trade centre. I was not able to visit Kokenhauf but the priest and family friends took me to a seaside flower show where dozens of profusely flower-decked vehicles took part. There were large colourful fields of tulips and lilies on the way.

My priest landlady took the trouble to take me for a violin concert in the opera house one evening. We took the city bus to and fro. Unfortunately, I was dressed in summer get-up and shivered all through the rides. The opera house was warm enough and I saw a few Indian faces too in the audience. I am not knowledgeable about classical Western music, but found the pieces soothing. More than the music it was the audience that impressed me.

There was pin-drop silence in the audience(unlike in my country) while the musicians played, but when the musicians finished the audience stood to give full applause. After each piece, the musician went backstage only to return and take bows as the audience clapped for encores. I remember there were more women than men among the musicians.

The two technicians I interacted with the most at the institute were Mareena, a Surinamese immigrant and Roeselyn the descendent of Jewish immigrants. Surinam was a colony of Holland and the Surinamese have special consideration in Holland's immigration policy. Mareena was short, brown and plump and looked almost like a South Indian matron. She was a very pleasant person and her usual dress was Bermuda shorts and T-shirts. I wistfully thought about how inhibited and conservative I was in matters of dressing. Mareena took me out one day, treated me to ice cream and insisted on buying me leggings to wear in Amsterdam.

Roeselyn was taller than the generally tall male population and was strikingly attractive. She was very good at her job, had a wide world view and understanding. She reminded me of the highly intelligent Jewish European women scientists mentioned in the later chapters. Roeselyn told me she changed boyfriends when the relationship lost its excitement. It was degrading and demeaning to keep a boyfriend if the sight of him stopped making her heart beat faster. Her current boyfriend was a professional football player. Though I have internalised patriarchal ideas of morality I do not feel called upon to pass judgement on the personal autonomy of this beautiful young European girl representing her generation. What is admirable is that youngsters like her are open about their relationships and do not have clandestine affairs and are not hypocritical.

Navroz took me to visit her family that was settled in a small village near the Netherland -Germany border that could be reached by a two-hour train journey from Amsterdam Central. Her family consisted of her mother, an older unmarried brother and a younger sister. I bought some yellow roses for the mother and she was really touched. She was a soft-spoken lady who told me in her hesitant English how she missed her country and its warm climate. I don't remember the brother's job, but he was surprisingly well informed about Kerala and Malayali Christians. The sister who worked in a shop told me how she had become nervous of turbaned Indian men after an incident when she was alone in the shop. Apparently, a sardarji entered the shop and insisted on telling her fortune in spite of her declining the offer. After uttering some unfamiliar words, he demanded five dollars and went away only after she gave him the money.

My trip to Europe was after our own easter celebration in India, but the Syrian Orthodox church in Holland celebrates it a few days later. I accompanied Navroz and the family to their church attached to a monastery for the easter service and met several of its members there. The church provided boiled eggs and chocolates to the attendees after service to break their easter Sunday fast. I was introduced to Navros's uncle who happened to be the monk in charge. He obligingly handed me a few dollars which I later gifted to Navroz who needed it more than me. She was instrumental in finding me free lodging and did not appear to be affluent. I also met a Malayalee Orthodox Bishop who was a guest at the monastery.

I had always doubted my Syrian ancestry but was surprised to see some of the elderly ladies who had the face and figures that reminded me of several acquaintances in Kerala and even some of my relatives. I think there is some degree of middle-eastern genetic mix in the Nasrani community to which I belong.

The priest's wife took me to a settlement of Syrians once. They stayed in small inexpensive newly built government flats and mostly worked in hotels and restaurants as cleaners or construction workers. They were trying to fit into the European lifestyle but felt the concealed antagonism in the original Hollanders. They were not fully at home but seemed reconciled to this feeling of alienation. All of them were trying to ensure the education of their children and hoping for a better future for them. These immigrants seemed acutely aware that they were resented by the native Hollanders. It is a fact we have to accept that the local population everywhere generally feels threatened by the influx of those who look and speak differently from them. This is especially true if the newcomers' religion is also alien. Malayalee's conflicted attitude to the influx of large numbers of workers from northeast India to Kerala is an example even though they belong to the same country. We need their labour capacity but feel nervous about the social impact of the intrusion. Europe is now in the grip of the social impact of immigration according to media reports.

My next sojourn was in the small German town of Bad Oeynhausen (B O for short) in Westphalia which has the famous Diabetic and Heart centre with organ transplantion facility. Reverend Koruth hailing from Kolenchery had arranged my programme and stay here. He was an Orthodox priest married to a German doctor and settled in Germany. Their son Johan picked me up from the railway station and drove me to my destination. I had the opportunity to admire the perfection of German construction as we drove along Hitler's autobahn. These roads were constructed mostly for troop movement during the war, but they are still in good condition.

I was given a room free of rent in the hostel attached to a convent close to the diabetic centrum. During my stay in the convent for more than two weeks I never saw a single nun around. Both male and female nurses attached to the hospital stayed at the hostel. I have a very vivid memory of a man who had murdered his wife also being accommodated there. He was on bail and was required to do social service in the hospital as part of his bail obligation. He came to my door once and invited me in his broken English to share beer and sausages. I escaped with the lame excuse that I was an Indian and both beer and sausages were anathema to Indians. I think he was already drunk and believed me. In the night the fellow went around banging on all the doors screaming and waking everyone. When I opened the door hearing the racket he was outside in the passage shouting incoherently. Other hostel inmates went in and locked their doors. The only impulse that came over me was to shout at him 'Go To Bed' repeatedly. To my surprise, the man turned quietly and went to his room. Maybe the memory of being told about Indians being vegetarians and teetotallers surfaced in his foggy mind and sobered him a little to realise his inappropriate behaviour. The other hostel members must have complained about him to whoever sent him there because he disappeared by morning and was never seen there again.

Bad Oeynhausen was a really pretty place. Rows of neat-looking houses with well-maintained lawns and well-tended gardens lined paved streets. I hardly saw people on the road or outside these houses. There was a silent church, a silent village museum and a neat park with leafy trees, a duck pond and beds of red and yellow tulips. I never saw a single person in the church or park. The village museum displayed ancient agricultural implements and the model of an old time farm house. When I visited it there was a lone young girl visiting it and no staff. A supermarket and railway station were within walking distance of the hospital. The only places where I saw small crowds were the two main streets lined by various shops. European visitors must be getting a cultural shock to witness our streets and shops teeming with people. All these places were within walking distance of the hostel.

Language plays a significant role in how comfortable a visitor feels in a country. I must confess to feeling isolated and not very comfortable in Germany mostly because of communication problems. The only words I knew were Danke (thanks), banhauf (railwaystation), and autobahn (road). In my experience, the German people do not like to speak English even when they know the language. The weather was cold and I felt even the people were cold. Sometimes I felt they were very insular in their attitude to the outside world of which they seemed to know very little. There are small incidents that linger in my memory.

The day after I reached BO the hospital staff members told me the only place to buy English newspapers was the railway station. So, armed with a map, I set out but soon got confused. The only people I saw on the road were a man and a woman coming from the opposite direction halfway through my journey. I greeted them and asked for directions. The man started to say something, but the woman grabbed him and pulled him back physically. I was left to wonder if I had the appearance of a woman terrorist for the lady to get so frightened.

The weather was colder than in Amsterdam and I needed extra socks. So, I went to a textile shop on the main road. They obviously had socks on the shelf, but the saleswoman could only repeatedly say no, no, no. Thankfully when I went to another shop close by the man in charge who spoke a little English not only sold me socks but kindly showed me how to find the correct fit by measuring one's closed fist. It seemed German women were more insular or anxious than their men.

There were also pleasant and sometimes entertaining experiences. To the natives used to the cold climate beginning of May is early summer. But I was feeling intensely cold as I was strolling on the main street one afternoon. The constant cold breeze added to my misery. So, I got into a small clothes store and asked for a warm scarf. The sales lady was sympathetic but told me they had withdrawn all winter clothing from the store as the winter was ending and replaced them with summer wear. But seeing how cold I appeared she fished around and found me a thick scarf with floral pattern. I gratefully wrapped it around my neck and immediately felt better. I think the shop was a one-woman enterprise and she sold homemade chocolates in the shop. Buying some and eating them all on the spot made me feel even better. It was the first time I truly believed in the power of the flavonoids in cocoa to raise the mood-stabilising neurotransmitters serotonin and dopamine. So, we wished each other pleasant goodbyes and I left. This scarf remained with me for several years.

There was a moderately expensive supermarket about three hundred metres away from my hostel. The staff and customers spoke only German and I used sign language. Customers had to take their shopping trolley only after inserting a five-mark coin in its side pocket. After billing and paying the customer could take it back. When I went to get a trolley the first time one employee came over caught the handle and said something in German. I stared at him uncomprehendingly and spoke in English. He kept talking in German. We were attracting the curiosity of people in the queue and I was getting embarrassed. Did this shop serve only whites? Then a sweet old lady who reminded me of Miss Marple of Agatha Christie's stories left the queue and came over. She explained the five-mark routine in broken English and showed me how to do it.

I had to be thrifty with my traveller's cheques and stretch them to last me till I went back home. Food was expensive and I had to plan my diet for maximum value for money. So, my diet consisted of different types of buns, boiled eggs, bananas and an inexpensive unflavoured yogurt. In fact, this was my routine diet plan throughout my two-month stay in Europe except on the occasions I was invited by friends or colleagues for a meal. It was monotonous but nutritionally balanced.

In the medical ward, I met a plump and kind black female nurse who rushed to catch me in a big friendly hug saying "poor you" very sympathetically. The reason for her pity was she had visited Chennai some years ago. Her overwhelming memory of India was that people were homeless and lived on the street. I did not try to explain I was far from homeless though homelessness was not very uncommon in India till the beginning of twenty first century.

My visit was during the time Europe was in the grip of fear about Bovine Spongiform Encephalopathy (BSE-mad cow disease) being transmitted to humans by beef consumption. BSE is a prion disease that has no cure and European countries were slaughtering cows on suspicion of BSE. I was astounded when a nurse told me that India wanted to import the cattle Germany was culling to feed the starving Indians. Then I recollected a newspaper report that quoted Uma Bharathi, a well-known politician, who offered to look after the cows Europe wanted to slaughter if they could be sent to India. The nurse's story showcases Europe's outdated understanding of modern India where cows are venerated to some extent, but in a practical manner. Also, unlike in colonial India, we no longer have starving millions in need of diseased cow meat, but sometimes glitches do occur in the public distribution system in remote areas affecting food availability.

The Diabetic and Heart Centre was a medium-sized modern building about half the size of my own hospital. The Diabetes department team had four male doctors and one lady doctor. They were ably assisted by a team of nurses, dieticians and a podiatrist. None of the doctors had ventured out of Europe and did not seem keen to know much about the rest of the world. But they were really single-minded and focused on their profession. In Germany, it takes longer for a medical student to qualify as a doctor than in India and even longer to become a postgraduate consultant. One doctor asked me if I was surprised to see such a big modern building as theirs. I told him we had bigger buildings in India and in my own state. His expression made it clear he did not believe me. I had no pictures of my institution to show him and left him to his conviction.

Title: River Werre

Cherry Tree in Blossam

The only lady doctor in the team was more open to the outside world. She was a blonde beauty in her thirties who had travelled in other European countries. She took me out to dinner at an Italian restaurant one evening. While I ate pasta with shrimp she was happy to munch on a large plate of leafy salad. The cook came over to ask what I thought of the dish I was eating and was happy I liked it. The doctor obviously was able to speak Italian and was a regular customer. It was not dark yet when we finished dinner. So, she took me to see their apparently famous local river(River Werre). I come from a land of numerous charming streams with clear water tinkling musically over pebbles and larger stately rivers and backwaters. I gaped at the small muddy stream that passed off as a river and tried not to look disappointed. Maybe it becomes wider and deeper as it flows. She was such a kind lady and was trying to make me feel at home.

There were innovative clinical studies going on in the diabetic centre. What was admirable and worthy of emulation was the earnestness and thoroughness they showed in their work. We in India generally tend to be rather casual and carefree in comparison. The podiatric section was an example. The diabetic footwear we supply our patients who have sensory loss and foot deformity is made with no consideration of weight bearing and pressure dynamics of the foot altered by deformity. We expect the patient's foot to adapt to the nonspecific uncomfortable footwear we supply even now. But even in those days, this centre made personalised foot wear after making casts of the foot to map out the pressure points and make appropriate shoes for individual patients. They also had a diabetic foot surgeon exclusively for foot care of diabetic patients. One interesting thing about this gentleman was he was a great believer in the ancient leech therapy for draining pus collection rather than incising the abscesses. It was a gruesome sight to see patients with half a dozen leeches attached to and feasting on their legs. The thread-like parasites would gorge on the pus and gradually swell up to finger size before falling off the leg. Leeches were commercially available in medical shops.

Insulin pumps still in the experimental stage had just arrived in the market and the Institute was trying them out on some young patients with Type 1 diabetes at the time. Type 1 diabetes patients are usually young and have serious deficiency of Insulin rather than Insulin resistance found in the generally older population of Type2 patients. Western countries have a larger proportion of Type 1 patients when compared to India. Young Indians tend to develop visceral obesity even without general obesity and consequent Insulin resistance earlier than their Western counterparts. This leads to Type 2 Diabetes. The ability to store energy as fat in the abdomen was an evolutionary advantage for populations in areas prone to famines like in colonial India. There are studies suggesting famines brought about by thoughtless British policies genetically modified Indian metabolism and promoted this adaptive mechanism. Now that food, especially carbohydrates, is plenty and famines non-existent this proneness to visceral fat accumulation is making India the capital of visceral obesity, insulin resistance and type 2 diabetes.

The Transplant programme was innovative too. I was told patients who needed kidney or heart transplant were admitted to the unit during skiing season in anticipation of accidental deaths among young people. I presume they have stringent criteria and supervision to avoid any malpractice. Organs were harvested without any delay or fuss once brain death was confirmed and transplanted as required. One may think this morbid, but it is an example of German pragmatism. The German doctors with their no-nonsense approach reminded me of the Chinese delegates I had seen at international conferences. They seemed unemotional and very focussed. The youngsters who survived with major disability were rehabilitated in the attached rehabilitation centre. It was a saddening sight to see young and otherwise healthy young men whizzing past on motorised wheelchairs.

One day a pastor of the local church came to the hospital and invited me to have dinner at his home. He was a friend of Rev Koruth who probably asked him to invite me. He and his wife came to escort me to their home one evening and plied me with rice, Chicken, some kind of bread and war stories. He spoke about his unhappy Nazi past in the second world war. He was a young man of eighteen when the war started and was enrolled in Hitler's army. Hitler apparently was a magnetic orator who could mesmerise his listeners and that is how all the young people were practically hypnotised and inspired to become soldiers of his Reich. He was captured and was a war prisoner of the allies for some years. After release he became remorseful and chose the spiritual path to make amends.

I had the opportunity to interact with the Malayalee diaspora over the two weekends I spent in Germany. On these two occasions, two couples who were members of the Malayalee Samajam took the trouble to come over and take me to their family homes. Both were happy homes and the couples were admirable hosts. The ladies were senior nurses Shiny and Molly(names changed). Shiny's husband was a male nurse and the other one's an engineer. On one occasion I attended the Orthodox Malayalam service presided over by Father Koruth with them. It was inspiring to hear the small children born and brought up in Germany reading out passages from the Malayalam Bible. But the service was excruciatingly long and it was impossible to be attentive for the two hours of prayer. The services in Kerala churches take only about one hour making it easier to be attentive.

The next weekend Shiny and her husband took me to see an old castle with a weather vane and a park with flowering rhododendrons. I remember seeing a white teenage girl sitting and crying on the steps of the castle. Nobody paused to ask her the reason and we too walked away. That night we attended the evening Malayalam Samajam party and met several members. They all seemed well off and comfortable in their jobs. But I think the first generation at least still felt a sense of alienation from mainstream German society.

With economic reforms, the whole world has become what we call the global village. In addition to job seekers, Germany has taken in refugees from the Middle East. It is an aging society with too many old people who need to be looked after and not enough young people to work. Now in the 2020s large numbers of Indians especially Malayalees are flocking to this country. So, this seemingly closed society is likely to become more open and pluralistic. Who can predict how painful it's going to be or if this process is good for the country or not? There are troubling reports of immigrant problems coming out of European countries now.

After two and a half weeks of stay, I bid goodbye to Bad Oeynhausen and Germany with mixed feelings. The time I spent there definitely gave me useful experience. People except the two women mentioned were kind to me. They seemed earnest and hard working. But still, the impression of Germans being an unhappy people remained with me. I had not found the ease and laughter that came so naturally to the people I met in Amsterdam in spite of their busy lives. My lack of knowledge of the German language and their inability or unwillingness to speak English had probably played a part in my not feeling completely at home in Germany.

Father Koruth was kind enough to send Johan to drive me to the Railway station to board the train back to Amsterdam Central. I had to organise all the laboratory materials and literature I had collected at the RTI and take leave of the friends who had been so helpful and kind to me in Amsterdam. In another two days, I would be bidding farewell to the beautiful city of flowering cherry trees, canals flanked by stately old buildings and friendly people. Navroz took me to Schiphol airport. I was startled to meet one familiar face at the launch. Mr Joy Jacob a confectioner and son of Mr Chacko Pillai who was closely associated with MOSC had landed there after a conference in France. He was on a business trip to Europe and had come to visit Kaukenhauf, the centre of floriculture and flower trading in Holland. I felt regretful I had not visited Kaukenhauf myself and promised myself a visit sometime in the future. (I still have not kept this promise to myself). I bid him and Navroz goodbye and boarded the flight to Heathrow to complete the last leg of my tour.

Dr Everard my mentor in Europe had some Indian mix in his ancestral tree and he was familiar with India. He had worked in the West Indies for most of his professional life. Though in his eighties, he actively followed up new developments in leptospirosis research. He met me at Heathrow Airport and took the trouble to drive me all the way to the Hereford County Hospital where the Leptospira reference centre was located to finish the last leg of my study tour in Europe. We drove through the open Welsh countryside along narrow roads flanked by meadows dotted with hedges and scattered clumps of trees. I remember some parts of the road running alongside a stream with banks covered with blue bells. Cows were grazing in some of the meadows. There was light rain throughout our journey.

I had expected the British people to be a strong and fierce race to have conquered India and subjugated its people for two hundred years. Instead, the average Briton I saw on the streets of England was of average physique and rather meek and timid looking. Obviously, brains and deviousness scored over brawn or affluence and modern comforts have subdued their conquering spirit.

Hereford, where the Leptospira reference centre was situated, had a calm rural atmosphere. The Leptospira laboratory was situated in a two-story building attached to the county hospital. The laboratory had four technicians, a microbiologist and a medical doctor in charge. Martin the microbiologist took on the duty of finding accommodation for me and helping me learn about their work. The number of clinical cases they had and samples tested were nowhere near the dozens of samples and mild to very severe cases of leptospirosis we had to deal with in Kolenchery. Still the lab had the facility for doing ELISA and MAT and the staff were helpful and cooperative. There were not many cases of leptospirosis in the area and they had not seen the havoc it could cause in a farming community. To them, it was a mild tropical illness easily treated with oral Doxycycline (A member of Tetracycline antibiotic family effective in early leptospirosis and also used as prophylaxis against it.)The Institute was intended for dealing with the few tropical diseases British tourist would bring back after visiting the tropics rather than solving the health problems of tropical countries.

Hereford had several budget housing projects. I was to lodge with a young woman in one of them. She was teaching in a junior school and her boyfriend was working in the construction industry. The rent for a bed and breakfast was very reasonable. Their two-bedroom duplex, one-bathroom house was on a small hillock named Grandison Rise. There was infrequent bus service from Grandison Rise to the Institute which was a kilometre away. I chose to walk the distance without waiting for the uncertain bus service. I often met young children playing on the road and some of them used to call out greetings. It was a genteel but not prosperous neighbourhood. All these factors along with ease of communication, unhurried traffic and the red post boxes on the road side as in India made me feel right at home. The land lady was an agreeable person too. I could make myself breakfast with whatever was available in her small kitchen. One evening she made me a dinner of cottage pie. I rarely saw the boyfriend. They were obviously not very prosperous and were trying to sell the house and migrate to London for a better future. One day she wanted to drive me to the Institute. We started and a few metres down the road the car started making banging sounds. The poor lady had to abandon the plan and call a mechanic. It was an old car in poor condition.

The roads were usually in good condition, but I had seen potholed ones too on the ninety-mile drive from London to Hereford. In general, the countryside was picturesque, genteel and pretty, but did not have impressive signs of prosperity. I remember passing a cider manufacturing unit on my daily walk to the hospital. The cities must have been busier and more I prosperous. I only had passing glimpses as we were driving through London. What did make an impression on me in those days was the bright rainbow-coloured hair of children with backpacks walking to school. Parrot green, ultramarine blue, ice-cream pink were all represented. Now we see heads of many colours in any small town in Kerala, but it was a novelty to me twenty-five years ago. Some of the boys and girls would be passionately kissing while striding along in their school uniform with school bags on their backs. The sight was mundane but because of my medical background, I did wonder if schools gave the young children adequate sex education about teen pregnancy and sexually transmitted diseases. The strongly conservative moral police cry foul when the topic is mentioned in Kerala but we need to empower children with knowledge of sexuality and procreation along with other life skills and social realities.

Dr Everard and his wife came over to drive me back to Calne, Wiltshire where they had settled after retirement. I stayed with them overnight. My flight to Chennai was scheduled for the evening the next day. They took me to see some of the historic places and relics around Wiltshire in the afternoon. The prehistoric carving of the chalky white horse on the side of the Cherhill and the many burial mounds from the bronze age at Seven Barrows are two sights I remember. We had tea and English muffins at the local pub. The general ambience was one of calm, peace and contentment. This old establishment tallied with my mind's image of old English pubs gathered from reading numerous

English classics. The evening was spent cooking. The Everards made a supposedly Indian curry with eggplant and chicken for my benefit. I reciprocated by teaching them to make chapati. The couple had made great efforts to make me feel at home and my study visits successful. The only disappointment again was the small stream that flowed on the side of their land. To me, it was a small muddy stream, but the Everards distinguished it by the name River Marden. It must have been a bigger stream earlier in the day with strong currents because there was a dilapidated windmill a little distance upstream. I remember they had a lone apple tree in bloom and a flowering poppy plant in their garden of which he was very proud.

The poppy plant with Dr Everard

The next afternoon Dr Everard drove me to Heathrow's check-in counter which was not busy. It was "womanned" by a smart black girl who asked me if I understood English and then put me through routine questions about my luggage and advised me not to accept any baggage from strangers. I was sad to finish my very satisfying study tour, but anxious to reach my home and family. Dr Everard and I shook hands and I walked on. That was the last I saw of this kind very Indian English gentleman. Dr Everard's wife became ill not long after and he could not travel anymore.

CHAPTER 10

VISITING THE LAND OF CANAAN

$\mathcal{F}$or many Christians, visiting the Holy land that witnessed Jesus's life and mission is a cherished dream. Because growing up in traditional practising Christian households naturally makes young minds form lasting images of Jesus, His birth, life and crucifixion. I was no exception and had my own inner images of Jesus and the events of His life. As a believer, I too wanted to experience the ambience of the Holy Land and picture Jesus roaming it on foot, meditating, healing, preaching and finally facing unimaginably cruel and unjust suffering. My husband, also a believer, and I joined a tour group visiting Israel in December 2017. There were about thirty people in the group consisting of three catholic priests, families of earnest Christian pilgrims and a lone Hindu lady interested in ancient archaeology of the Middle East.

The Emirate flight from Kochi and subsequent arrangements were fairly comfortable. We transited in Bahrain and flew into Queen Alia airport in Jordan by noon. We checked into a hotel in the city for an overnight stay and short sightseeing trips.

The afternoon before crossing into Israel was spent visiting a curio shop and Mount Nebo, the hilltop from where Moses surveyed the promised land of Canaan to which he was leading his rebellious mob. The Bible says he did not reach Canaan but Yahweh granted him a view of the panorama of the promised land before he died. The rather arid-looking vista of the land of Canaan (parts of which form Israel) rolls out before one's eyes from this high view point above the Jordan valley. It is easy to imagine Moses standing atop the crest of Mount Nebo and gazing across the valleys and hills beyond he was not destined to enter. He must have been very tired.

Stone engravings and a pillar stand atop the hill in tribute to this great Jewish hero and his epic journey out of Egypt. There were several pilgrim groups visiting the site and most were making a beeline to stand and get photographed near the serpentine cross on the crest of the mount. The Italian sculptor Giovanni Fantoni who crafted this unusual cross is considered to have been inspired by the gospel verse John3:14 which links the brass serpent Moses raised in the wilderness and faith in the Son of Man for salvation. The never-ending saga of conflicts and wars that haunted and continues to haunt Israelite's promised land has made it a place where human blood rather than milk and honey flow.

Serpentine Cross at Mt Nebo

There is a Church built over the remains of an old Byzantine church at Nebo. When we reached it, a service by another pilgrim group was in progress. We did not go inside but only stood at the open door. The apse of the church has some mosaics recovered from the ruins of the fourth-century Byzantine church.

We left Jordan to cross into Israel by road the next morning. The only bad memory of our brief Jordan halt is of the terrible toilets at the Jordan Israel border before crossing into Israel. We walked across to the Israeli immigration office for checking and afterwards were met by a tall military-looking middle-aged lady. She was a Jewish immigrant from Ukraine and was efficient and business-like. She managed the tour group very efficiently for the next eight days. Somehow the tour group was rather nervous of her and started calling her Maggie Aunty in a good-humoured manner behind her back. The immigration checking at the border crossing was strict, professional and efficient, carried out in solemn silence.

The tour was during the week before Christmas and Bethlehem was rather cold and getting ready to celebrate Christmas. A huge Christmas tree was already erected in front of the Nativity Church. We were to be based at a mid-level hotel called Ben Hur in Bethlehem and go on trips by bus to the different sites on our itinerary. Israel is a country smaller than our small Indian state of Kerala and easy to crisscross, but so many relics of history are crammed into this little strip of land.

Christmas in Bethlehem

I remember Israel more as a Biblical museum rather than the prosperous country it is and my trip was a pilgrimage and a study tour combined. There are so many sites of historic significance and scenes of ancient drama that one loses count of them in a short visit. Most of them have not been excavated and studied. Israel was inhabited at least by 3000 bc and has been invaded and conquered by many empires. Conflict and violence continue till today. When we visited there was apparent peace on the surface but a transient visitor cannot assess the undercurrent of antagonism between Jews and Palestinians.

Ashkelon, an ancient city of Israel excavated in 1985, showed evidence of almost ten civilisations in the unearthed fifty feet of rubble. The relatively fertile northern part and the semi-arid south have been equally attractive to invaders and settlers. Maybe its reputation of untold riches and easy accessibility through the Mediterranean Sea made it irresistible to invaders. The present-day Israel is a far cry from the old vulnerable land and people. It is a tiny country in a hostile neighbourhood managing to flourish and appear as a desirable and peaceful enough tourist destination. But conflicts occur from time to time making peace prospects unpredictable.

Israel excels in modern technology in manufacturing, defence and agriculture. Israel's highly effective use of water, characterised as liquid gold is maximised by recycling, desalination and judicious irrigation methods like micro irrigation should be an exemplary model other arid lands can copy. As we travel by road through the mostly brown landscape we see blooming agricultural pockets of plantain, citrus, dates and olive groves. The roads were smooth and easy to drive along. There were no traffic jams on these roads probably because of our trip organiser's correct timing to avoid busy traffic hours. There were occasional sightings of colourfully adorned camels at the roadside. The towns we passed had modern multistorey buildings interspersed with old handsome classic buildings. We saw small white houses at regular intervals. Most of these houses had citrus bushes laden with oranges in the front. The olive trees looked like shrubs and had small black fruits. We resisted the temptation to stop the bus and steal some of the luscious fruits.

Some sights certainly impressed more and stood out. The monuments and holy relics are preserved and maintained beautifully. Even the ruins are well-kept in their natural state. The country gains sizable income from tourism apart from high-tech agriculture, manufacturing and diamond export. Over the centuries Jews have displayed great resourcefulness to exploit opportunities and flourish even in the midst of the harsh treatment meted out to them in most countries they have inhabited. This quality has made them stand apart in different societies they lived in and elicited enmity, jealousy and persecution. It is remarkable that India is the only country that did not persecute Jews when they were refugees here. Our land has always graciously accepted refugees and this fact accounts for the great diversity in ethnicity and culture we see in modern India. Today this tiny country of Israel can vie with any of the developed nations in terms of per capita income, living standard and defence.

It is recorded by the historian Bishop Eusebius that the geographical sites where different biblical events took place were identified by Queen Helena, the mother of Roman emperor Constantine in the fourth century. Whether she was born as a Christian or was converted later is not clear. But Bishop Eusebius states that she took a two-year-long pilgrimage of Palestine with a large entourage when she was in her seventies. She identified the sites of important events in the life of Jesus after interacting with local people and familiarising herself with local history and geography. She is said to have discovered fragments of the true cross Jesus was crucified on. The queen was also the moving force behind building important early churches like the Church of Nativity, the Church of Eleona on mount Olive and the Church of Holy Sepulchre. There is no way anyone can contest her findings unless excavations are done in all these areas to prove or disprove them. Israel has meticulously preserved these sites.

There were a few narratives about events and sites described to us by the guide that challenged my ability to believe. The Church of St Joseph in Nazareth has a large covered box-sized crypt that the guide told us was the saint's workshop. We went to Bethany where Jesus's much loved friends Martha, Mary and Lazarus lived. An underground chamber with steep steps was described as the tomb of Lazarus from which Jesus raised him. Many of us in our early old age climbed down to it with some effort. Another surprise was when the guide took us to an ancient covered well on Mount Sinai and told us it was Moses's well. A well-trimmed creeper nearby was pointed out to us as the burning bush of Moses in which angel of the Lord appeared to Moses. The bush was green in December but is said to turn to flame colour in fall. These may be based on myths or facts, it is difficult to say. But they do no harm to anyone and so should be left alone.

On several occasions, we were taken to curio shops where the sales people displayed irresistible and compelling sales techniques. Some in our hapless group (maybe it was jetlag) ended up with art pieces they did not particularly want. We had a similar experience when we were taken later to a perfume shop in Cairo. The chief salesperson was a middle-aged man who claimed he was a Bedouin alchemist who explored the Judean desert for rare raw materials to produce mysterious fragrances. He was very chivalrous and flattered the ladies profusely. He promised us that his perfumes could enhance a woman's seductive allure. Understandably our middle-aged and elderly group did not show much interest in the art of seduction. He had two lady assistants who kept dabbing perfumes on our wrists after he displayed each container. Our group twittered and giggled politely, but I don't know if any bottle was sold. I think it was a case of overkill on the salesman's part.

Touring groups were allowed free access to all the churches and could perform services conveniently. The priests leading our group carried out services and prayers at most of the important sites. There were pilgrims of all colour, age and nationality at most of these sites, all of them devoutly praying or chanting or taking pictures. We hardly saw any locals at these places. We also witnessed a long line of Asian-looking devotees being baptised by immersion in the river Jordan by their priest. The only places we came across Jewish people were shops, hotels, via dolorosa and the wailing wall.

We were able to visit many of the holy places, but there must be a lot more to see and understand about Israel than we did in this short span of our visit. However, the place that cast a spell over me was mount Tabor where transfiguration of Christ is said to have happened.

We started the trip to Mount Tabor before dawn broke and reached the mount before any other group reached there. Tabor is a small hill rising to about 450 metres above sea level. The air was cool on our faces as we drove up the narrow road winding along the wooded hill side and stopped outside the gate of the Church of Transfiguration. There was absolute silence. A rough stone path leading up to the Church of Transfiguration is flanked by what I remember as a magical garden. Bleached stones irregularly arranged as walls had colourful flowers rising out of earthen pots on them. Remnants of a ruined abbey also made up parts of the small but lovely garden. There were flowering shrubs and cacti peeping out of the abbey ruins. A bust of Antonio Barluzzi who was the architect of this Franciscan church is also in the garden. The church was already open and our priests started conducting morning service. I missed most of the service because I was lost in the magic of the place and the small garden. I can only say I experienced moments of spiritual upliftment. I could well imagine Peter, James and John being bedazzled enough by this mount of mystic energy to propose building tents for Jesus, Elijah and Moses. Rationalists do not believe in what cannot be proven. But I believe there are more forms of energy in the universe science is yet to identify. Think of the time before Benjamin Franklin discovered electricity. Scientific advancement in the distant future will dismiss or prove many of our unproven beliefs.

More groups started arriving as we were leaving the premises. The magical moments were gone.

The site that contrasted sharply with my mind's image was the mount of Beatitudes and Sermons. I always imagined a sharp grassy slope where the multitude sat listening intently to Jesus's words of wisdom. To face the large crowd directly and speak to them Jesus got into the wooden rocking boat which must have been steadied by the disciples. I was surprised by the hardly noticeable slope on the shore of Galilee and asked the guide where the hill was. She said we were standing on the mount. However, the green grounds and attached buildings were impressive though they failed to ignite my imagination.

One afternoon was spent visiting Mount Olive situated in the At-Tur district of Jerusalem. There is a Carmelite monastery and the Pater Noster church amidst the ruins of the fourth-century Byzantine church of Eleona, built by Queen Helena. The tomb of princess Aurelia Bossi who tried to complete restoration of the church of Eleona is also here. (There are several other churches too on the mount Olivet). The surrounding garden is mostly of shrubs and trees and not particularly beautiful. Probably it was not their flowering season. The walls of all the constructions are covered with plaques displaying the Lord's prayer in over a hundred languages including Malayalam. Looking across the Kidron Valley from the mount we could see the golden Dome of the Rock as well as the smaller dome of the church of Holy Sepulchre. The world is acutely aware of the conflicts and debates surrounding the Dome of Rock and the Islamic shrine within as well as the West Bank settlements. Everyone was silent as we climbed down the steep side of the hill to the Gethsemane garden. I think the impermanence of human life and our apparent human achievements must have occupied all our thoughts.

Gethsemane garden at the foot of Mount Olive is the scene of Jesus's agonised prayer in anticipation of forthcoming extreme suffering and where His disciples failed Him. The millennia old gnarled olive trees (or at least their ancestors) must have been witnesses to this heart-wrenching image in the minds of the faithful. The adjoining Church of All Nations is full of paintings depicting the Passion of Christ. It only had a few visitors when we entered the premises.

A Medley of Memories and Musings

Ancient olive tree in Gethsamene garden

We were taken to the side of the Gehenna valley above which the monastery of St Onuphrius under the Greek Orthodox church is situated. We looked down into the Potters field apparently bought with the betrayal money of Judas. Judas is said to have hanged himself here. The steep hillside is riddled with tombs and caves we were told. We were not allowed to visit the monastery.

Late afternoon we walked up the slope of the via Dolorosa (path of sorrow). The walk was sombre and memorable. We started at the foot of the old path where Jesus stumbled along carrying the wooden cross at least as heavy as Himself amidst the laughing, jeering crowd. I wondered what happened to the multitudes that used to come to listen to Him and to be healed. Why did they forget His words and deeds? Apparently, they were active participants in the crowd that tormented Him. I also remembered Simon the Cyrene who carried the cross for Jesus. Why is the Church silent about his role in providing the much needed relief to Jesus's suffering? Whether he was compelled by the soldiers to carry the cross or he did it out of kindness hardly matters. He did carry Jesus's cross and was the only person who ameliorated Jesus's suffering. The Cyrene deserves to be revered just as much as the disciples who deserted their teacher in His hour of suffering and ran away.

The road leading up to Golgotha known as Via Dolorosa (Path of Pain) is a moderate incline paved with stones and is less than a kilometre long. Both sides of the path are lined by small and large shops. We stopped and prayed at each station marked mostly by ancient-looking doorways in between old and new constructions. The road was crowded with pilgrim groups and local citizens. This was the only place in Israel where we saw several gun-wielding soldiers passing by. Some of the shopkeepers were calling out to the pilgrims. I saw an old shopkeeper calling out to our group –"good people of India, welcome".

Via Dolorosa

The last five of the fourteen stations are within the complex of the Church of Holy Sepulchre. The guide rushed us through as soon as we entered to the slight elevation called Golgotha where the cross was supposed to have been erected. We touched the floor through an opening in the centre of a star on the floor and joined the queue to enter the small enclosure purported to contain the tomb of Jesus. Whether historically accurate or not it was an emotionally charged moment for all of us as we entered the enclosure and touched the tomb within. Someone had anointed the tomb with perfume. Several ladies in our group had special scarves they had brought with them to wipe the tomb with great reverence. This was definitely the defining moment of our Israel trip.

We walked across to the crumbling western wall from via Dolorosa. Twilight was fading, but a great many people were sitting on the steps leading down to the wall. Many were rocking and chanting. Some were silent. Many were at the wall touching it. I too walked down to the wall. I had been told people could leave written prayer requests in the gaps between the ancient stones. The small gaps between the stones were packed with scraps of paper carrying people's heartfelt prayer requests. I too believe in the power of single-minded prayer. Whether prayers are answered through a divine external agency or by a process of subconscious self-empowerment is beyond my comprehension. But we are connected to the world around us by an intangible and ill-understood energy. I added my prayer request into a gap already stuffed with bits of paper. My prayer was granted in time.

Do I believe in miracles? Yes, I do. The natural events around us are all miraculous. To think of a simple example, a jackfruit seed contains all the exact DNA sequences programmed into the small seed to sprout, grow into a massive tree, withstand diseases, bear fruit and ultimately die. To me, this programming in all existence around us is the greatest of miracles. We do not think of them as miracles only because of our familiarity with them and our partial knowledge of the science behind them. If science matures in the distant future, miracles will disappear because the mechanics of what we now consider mysterious will be understood. By then human race would have evolved into an unimaginably intelligent and knowledgeable one. Events and natural phenomena will be anticipated, controlled or prevented. Sadly, the human capacity to marvel at miracles will also disappear alongside. However, at present, we need the humility to acknowledge that scientific knowledge is incomplete and still in the developing stage. I believe more forms of energy than we know of now exist including the energy of strong emotions. The fact that we are still ignorant about them is no reason to think they do not exist or cannot affect or modify natural events through still unknown processes.

The Marian Shrine and Milk Grotto in Bethlehem is another site where we came across touchingly emotional scenes of women weeping and praying. The Holy family is said to have halted in the cave briefly before fleeing to Egypt and legend has it that while feeding infant Jesus a few drops of milk fell in the cave turning it white. Women who have fertility problems come here to pray to Mother Mary, the symbol of Divine Motherhood. Ingesting lime stone powder from the cave and praying to the Mother is believed to help them conceive and many women testify to attaining motherhood thus. Air in the caves is cool and the atmosphere is serene.

Inside the Milk Grotto

Capernaum along the Sea of Galilee was the stage where Jesus performed many of the miracles described in the Gospels. There is a very modern-looking church close to the extensive ruins of what once must have been the town of Capernaum. The area was practically deserted as we walked to the seashore nearby. The sea looked gentle, deserted and placid. The shore was full of pebbles in the part where the group was led to. We could walk into the waveless sea without fear of getting drenched or carried away. The Sea of Galilee is hardly a sea and is actually a freshwater lake fed by river Jorden supplying precious water to Israel. We went further and boarded a fishing boat that took us on an hour-long ride in the gentle waters. Later we had lunch at an old-fashioned eatery called St Peter's Fish which gave us each a long fish fried whole to justify the name. It tasted insipid to us Malayalees who are used to highly spiced fish preparations at home. The only other visitors we saw were three silent black cats outside the eatery.

Visitors at the St Peters Fish

We spent a restful morning at the dead sea shore another day. There were many visitors frolicking in the water, but it was not too crowded. We saw only one couple floating far into the sea. Our middle-aged and oldish group was happy enough paddling in knee high or waist high water. Many of the ladies had bottles with them to collect some of the mineral rich dead sea mud to take back home as beauty aids and gifts for friends and relatives.

We could wash off the salt deposited on us at conveniently installed fresh water taps and showers along the shore.

I find it difficult to understand how so much hate and anger exist in the minds of people inhabiting this placid looking ancient land. October 7th, 2023 and the subsequent violence has shattered the happy images of Holy Land I kept in my mind.

The last two days of our tour were in Egypt. A friendly Egyptian called Abdul took charge of us at the Israel-Egypt border. Both our entry into Israel from Jordan and exit into Egypt took place at land borders and so we did not experience an Israeli airport. It would have been interesting. River Nile was sighted at several points during the bus journey. The sheer breadth of this river surprises one. After tumbling through forests and hills of almost a dozen African countries, the Nile in Cairo reminded one of a well-fed, rich and complacent matron. It seemed to have forgotten the arduous journey through multiple nations for thousands of kilometres of hills, mountains and forests and looked placid and still in the plains of Cairo.

We were driven to a fairly comfortable hotel in the outskirts of Cairo to relax. I don't remember the name of this hotel which had a large garden between the building and the beach. I think it was off-season because we did not come across many guests. The only guests we saw were an obviously Indian middle-aged couple the man wearing a dhoti and the lady in a burqa. I was curious about their presence but did not venture for an introduction. The hotel garden had shrubs and palm trees but hardly any flowering plants. The sea was within a short distance beyond the garden and we could hear the waves from the garden. Dinner was excellent and I remember we had fresh luscious dates for dessert. They were far more delicious than the dry dates we get to eat elsewhere. We retired early to bed to be ready for the next two days of hurried sightseeing. We would be flying out of Cairo in forty-eight hours.

The next day was spent visiting curio shops, a large papyrus factory, perfume shops and textile shops. All of us were eager to buy fine Egyptian cotton clothes for friends and relatives back home. We had been told Egyptian cotton was of extra fine quality. The papyrus factory truly amazed us with the manual art of transforming long reeds into papyrus sheets and finally into fine, delicate paper to be painted on by local artists. All of us bought these papyrus paintings with enthusiasm. They reminded us of our youthful days and history lessons in school of how Egyptians were one of the first people who manufactured paper and the term paper is derived from the name papyrus. (Google says Ts'ai Lun of China did it first). They showed us how the reed was processed to make paper.

We were also taken to the church Abi Serja built over the crypt where the holy family lived secretly after their flight from Herod who wanted to kill baby Jesus. There are beautiful paintings on the church wall as well as the underground crypt. There was an overpowering musty smell in the crypt. A protected well here claims to have supplied drinking water to the Holy Family in their hideout.

We were rushed out of the church by the guide apparently because there was some kind of violent disturbance close by. Someone informed our group that an extremist group had attacked and killed Coptic Christians somewhere nearby. However, the street outside looked deserted except for a young man who was trying to sell wall hangings to tourists.

All of us were looking forward to our visit to the Cairo Museum. It was an impressive building where we had to climb long rows of steps to view larger-than-life statues, sarcophagi, gold-plated chariots, ornaments and mummies of both humans and animals. However, to me, it was a sad place that reminded me of famines, deluges, plagues, human exploitation and wars. The rest of the group too seemed listless and our guide Abdul too became less enthused. I was thinking of the two powerful queens of Egypt Nefertiti and Cleopatra and expecting to learn something of their life and times. But there were no artefacts related to either of these two most famous of Egyptian queens. Apparently the authorities had moved out several important exhibits to other museums because the place was being rearranged. To my untrained eye, the display of exhibits and lighting seemed lacklustre. Some of the mummies were left open to the room air. The general ambience was one of decay and neglect. Maybe we were all tired and were not history enthusiasts.

The next day was spent in Giza visiting the great pyramids and the sphinx in the Nile valley close to Cairo. The large expanse of sand, crowds of ragged-looking persistent vendors all together are overwhelming. Some of us tried climbing up a short distance along the large stone blocks of the pyramid, but nobody was bold enough to try and enter the chamber. Subconscious fear of the unknown Pharaoh's curse must have held us back. However, we could not but marvel at the skill and effort that went into building these wonders rising so proudly against the cloudless sky. I know nothing about the GDP or economic health of Egypt, but the people we saw at these historic sites seemed abjectly poor. This must be the same impression tourists to India gain when they visit some of our own tourist spots. Just as in India, the overall economic situation in the country must be very different from the picture tourist spots present to visitors.

Egypt

Lunch was at an open cafe within calling distance of the Great Sphinx. I walked close enough to stare into its damaged face. The sphinx is believed to have been made around BC 2600 during the reign of Pharaoh Khafre and its face is said to have features similar to the king's. The facial disfigurement too has a story attached to it--The Nile valley used to be flooded in a cyclical manner destroying the farmers' crops. So, in 1378 the farmers worshipped and made offerings to the great sphinx to control the floods. This so offended the Sufi Muslim Saim al-Dhar that he destroyed the sphinx's nose. He was executed on charges of vandalism.

Our last evening in Cairo was spent attending a dinner party aboard a small ship anchored by the shore of the Nile. There were several Arab-looking persons including modern-looking couples. The food was indifferent, but the highlights of the evening were two dancers. A thin young voluminously clothed man performed the tanoura dance twirling a number of what seemed like colourful cloth umbrellas with great ease. A scantily clad pretty girl took the floor next and performed a dance with complicated hip and bust movements to instrumental music supplied by an all-male Troupe. It looked rather like belly dance to me. She looked quite comfortable with all the open male gaze. Both dancers were graceful and skilled to our untrained eye and all of us applauded and got photographed with them. I wondered later if we were expected to tip them, but the matter didn't occur to us at the time. On the other hand, they would have felt insulted by the offer of tips.

What impressed me at the party was the dress code of the native attendees. They all were in Western attire with the men sporting warm comfortable suits and tuxedoes and the ladies left to face the cold room in scanty clothing. Obviously, the compulsory

Islamic dress code was not enforced at the party. Egypt was more egalitarian in its treatment of women in the past compared to other civilisations according to historians. Vestiges of this liberal attitude obviously remain in their present-day society to some extent in spite of Islamisation. The recent ban on face cover for school girls is an example of this. The local women we saw selling trinkets near the pyramids were also unveiled and unself conscious. Our group had no particular dress code, only the casual comfortable every day clothes and did not face any stricture from authorities. This attitude of live and let live is admirable. Surprisingly we did not come across many other tour groups unlike in Israel.

We vacated the hotel after breakfast next morning to reach Cairo airport to catch the flight to Bahrain and onto Kochi and home. The trip was enjoyable and enlightening, but we were all anxious to reach home.

What did I learn from my much-anticipated visit to the holy land? There are sites like Mount Tabor, Gethsemane garden, via Dolorosa and Jesus's tomb that deeply move a believer in Jesus, but Israel is also a museum of past civilisations and their demise. The profusion of ruins and relics of human history crammed into this tiny country cannot but induce sombre contemplation. A visitor familiar with the history of this ancient land and its present state can only leave it with the thought that individual lives, societies, the human race, and civilisations that appear enormously significant and all important from our human perspective, are only minor parts in the ever-evolving drama at play in nature. Experiencing the holy land is to become sensitive to the transience and limited relevance of the human race in the total reality of the Universe and its recurring cycles of creation, destruction and recreation.

Time passes

www.ingramcontent.com/pod-product-compliance
Lightning Source LLC
LaVergne TN
LVHW061616070526
838199LV00078B/7299